The
Cat & Dog Lover's
IDEA BOOK

Gail Green

Published by

krause publications

The World's Largest Hobby and Collectibles Publisher

700 E. State Street • Iola, WI 54990-0001
715/445-2214 • FAX: 715/445-4087 www.krause.com

Please call or write for our free catalog of publications. Our toll-free number to place an order or obtain a free catalog is 800-258-0929 or please use our regular business telephone 715-445-2214.

Library of Congress Catalog Number 2001088591
ISBN 0-87349-216-1

The following registered trademark terms and companies appear in this publication:
Wool-Ease®, Jamie® (Lion Brand Yarn); Gem-Tac™ or Fabri-Tac™ Permanent Adhesive, CraftFoam Glue™ (Beacon™ Chemical Co.); Shaggy Plush Felt™, Rainbow Shaggy Felt™, Rainbow Classic™ Felt, FlashFelt™ (Kunin Felt, A Foss Manufacturing Company, Inc.); Gallery Glass® Window Color, Fashion® Dimensional and/or Brush-on Fabric Paint, Apple Barrel Colors®, Indoor Outdoor Gloss™, Folk Art® Outdoor Gloss Sealant, Decorator™ Glazes (Plaid Enterprises); Needleloft® Craft Cord (Uniek); Peel n Stick™ Double Sided Adhesive Sheet, HeatnBond™ Ultra Hold Iron-On Adhesive (Therm O Web). Stamped images used with permission 2001© Hero Arts Rubber Stamps, Saral Paper Corp., Wrights Trims, Zims, Inc., Fibre-Craft, Walnut Hollow, All Night Media, DMC© Embroidery Floss, "Naughty Puppy Cross-Stitch"© Janlynn Corp., Design Works, Fairfield Processing, Hampton Arts Rubber Stamps.

Acknowledgments

A word of thanks to my editors Amy Tincher-Durik and Christine Townsend, and all the wonderful dog and cat owners, handlers and experts whose animal models, photos, ideas, projects and collective wisdom made this book possible. And, most of all, a word of praise to the Creator who made us all.

Photographers: Jeff Green and Barb Zurawski.
Book cover photographry by In Focus Images, Jeff Green.

Contributors

Angela Stryck with Dancer and Venus
Lynn Adams with Hunter
Marilyn Manning with Vicky, Laurie and Tracy
Candy Kiiskila with Persians
Diana Antlitz
Gary and Susie Cohn with Stitchie and Patrick
Dee Coleman with Pogo
Linda Czuba with Riley
Bernard and Lee Danenberg
Peggy Farrell-Kidd with Phoebe
Lynn Glickauff with Roxann
Katie Green
Jeff and Lea Harris
Joe and Lynn Heidinger
Beth Ann Hill with Zane, Marin, Victoria, Obadiah, Jedidiah, Paige and others
Burt and Barb Horowitz with Rosie
Nirel Katz with Rascal
Carol Mazur with Pumpkin, J.J., and Star
Eileen Rosen and Sadie
Judy Roth with Wendy
Pat Schulz and Maureen Tobias with Devlin, Quinn and others
Diane Schroeder
Nancy Sugarman with Bear
Judy Wahrling with Susie and Gabby
Mary and Christy Wong with Jasmine
Linda Ziegler with Bailey, Presley and other Irish Setters
... and the author's best friends: Tyler, Shade and Suds

Photo permission In Focus Imagery, Jeff Green

Table of Contents

Photo
permission
In Focus Imagery,
Jeff Green

Introduction

Owning a pet is both a wonderful privilege and a great responsibility. Our timeless bond with animals is reflected in legacies such as a dog breed named after an English monarch (Cavalier King Charles Spaniel) or the wee terrier that was faithful to his master even after his master's death (the Scottish story entitled "Greyfriar's Bobby"). Family pets have appeared in paintings throughout the centuries. Dogs and cats have also inspired dozens of favorite stories, including *Puss In Boots* and *Lassie Come Home* … not to mention modern animation, television, and the movie industry.

The love affair we have with our pets has been steadily increasing in numbers and intensity. Many of us routinely leave the air conditioning, television, or radio on for our pet's benefit while we are at work. We buy special toys for them to play with, hire pet sitters, and give them gifts on special occasions. Instead of thinking of them as "just dogs or cats," many of us consider them members of our families. We love them in many of the same ways we would a child. How many dog bakeries, day care, and birthday party facilities have also sprung up in many parts of the country as a response to this desire to spoil our pets? As the majority of our population ages, more and more multiple pet households are appearing. These pets provide us with companionship in the absence of our grown children.

The unique abilities of dogs and cats also help us to defy our own limitations. Using their instincts, these animals can move herds of livestock, control vermin, or protect our families and possessions. They also aid the physically challenged, sniff out drugs or bombs, and help in the rehabilitation of both criminals and stroke victims. They comfort the lonely and teach our children to show kindness. This book is a celebration of this unique and often magical animal-human bond.

SEWING, STITCHING, AND CRAFT TECHNIQUES AND TERMS

Terms used for sewing
- RST (right sides together)
- WST (wrong sides together)
- RSO (right side out)
- WSO (wrong side out)
- Hand-tack: use a simple overcast stitch
- All machine stitching is done with a regular straight stitch, unless otherwise noted; use the appropriate needle and stitch if you are using knit material

Knitting terms
- CO = Cast On
- K = Knit
- P = Purl
- ST = Stitch
- INC = Increase 1 stitch in the next stitch
- K2 TOG = Knit 2 stitches together

To create a duplicate stitch
1. Take 1 or 2 small stitches on WS, leaving 1" of yarn loose.

2. Bring needle up through center of the base of the stitch, then under the 2 strands at the top of the stitch. Pull the yarn to the front **(Diagram A)**. Insert the needle back through the original point to complete the stitch.

Diagram A

3. Repeat these steps for each stitch, working horizontally or diagonally **(Diagram B)**. Tack loosely in place on WS.

To create stamps from craft foam
1. Attach press-on adhesive to WS of craft foam. Trace an image onto the foam, using a stylus or pen.

Diagram B

2. Cut the image out, remove the protective paper and attach to a mount, such as scrap wood. (Optional: Omit the press-on adhesive and glue images on to the mount instead. Let dry completely.)

To prepare project pattern pieces
The patterns found on pages 109-111 are used in multiple ways throughout this book. Some projects may require a pattern to be copied and enlarged per project instructions. To make your own patterns per instructions, measure carefully and transfer dimensions and/or shapes to large gridded interfacing, large sheets of tracing paper or clean paper grocery bags, opened up flat.

To prepare ceramic pieces for painting
1. Clean the plate with alcohol or vinegar. Rinse and dry completely with a clean towel.

2. Brush a light coat of bake-able varnish on the area where you will be painting. Let dry completely several hours or overnight.

How to measure your pet's neck
1. Place a tape measure around your pet's neck and insert fingers beneath the tape measure for comfort: one finger for small sizes, two fingers for medium sizes and three fingers for large sizes.

2. Add 1" to this measurement for elastic collars.

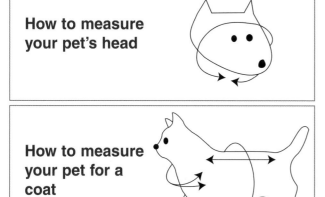

How to measure your pet's head

How to measure your pet for a coat

For all sewed collars attached with hook and loop tape:
1. Measure your pet's neck.

2. Add (2", 3", 4") inches to this measurement. Add 1" extra for collars made out of bulky fabrics, such as faux fur or Berber fleece.

3. Position the soft side of the tape on the project so that it will be on the side facing the animal's body, with the hook portion facing away.

General instructions for bandanas
(One yard of fabric makes 2 large, 4 medium or 6 small bandanas.)
1. Cut squares from fabric: 16" for small sizes, 22" for medium sizes and 30" for large sizes.

2. Cut each square in half on the diagonal.

3. Trim edges with pinking shears for non-sew projects, or press edges under and secure with fabric glue, iron-on adhesive, or by sewing.

Creating seam allowances
All seam allowances will need to be added to printed patterns but are included in all other pattern dimensions and/or instructions to create patterns. When stitching, allow a minimum of 1/2" seams on regular fabrics and 1" seams on bulky fabrics such as faux fur or Berber fleece *unless otherwise noted*. However, depending on your machine, the type or thickness of fabric, scale of project and sewing skills, seams can be wider or narrower if desired.

General notes on the projects contained in this book
● Unless otherwise indicated, most of these projects can be made for either a dog or cat.

● Cat collars should be made *only* with a breakaway clasp or hook and loop tape! Dog collars made with hook and loop closures or ribbon ties are for decorative purposes only and should not be used when containment is necessary.

● *All the toys in this book are to be used with supervision and are not intended for use by aggressive or destructive chewers.* Please check the condition of these toys often for wear or damage, and remove from access when early signs of damage are apparent.

● Offer treats sparingly to avoid digestive upset or weight gain. The treats in this book do not contain any preservatives; therefore, refrigeration and freezing are recommended.

● Unless otherwise indicated, all measurements and yardage information will be for sizes small, medium and large, indicated with commas and set off in parentheses. Example: (1", 2", 3"). These sizes are approximate and may have to be adjusted by measuring them against your pet. Smaller or larger sized pets, as well as proportionately different breeds, may require more or less yardage. Neck, length, waist or girth (chest) measurements may also vary proportionately, depending on the type of breed. For example, a Greyhound's neck size might be smaller than a Bulldog's for a collar. Both breeds could be the same length or girth for a jacket, but obviously require different sized beds.

● Double-check your patterns and/or collar measurements on your pet before cutting out the fabric, trims, and elastic, as well as the length and positioning of the hook and loop tape.

Chapter 1
MAKING DECISIONS

Research has shown that stroking a cat or petting a dog actually can reduce stress by lowering our heart rates and blood pressure. This pleasurable interaction also can have the same beneficial effect on our pets. (Courtesy Beth Ann Hill)

Choosing a Pet

A pet is a lifelong commitment, both of time, emotion and finances, and should not be chosen on impulse. Any animal that you take into your life deserves the time it takes to make sure it's the right one for your family. Before making a decision, consider the following:

1. Does everyone in the household want a pet? Are all in agreement as to whether a cat or dog is wanted?

The primary caretakers must be in agreement and want to take care of this new family member. It is both unfair and unwise to bring a dog or cat into a household in which it may not be wanted or possibly abused.

2. Are you willing to spend the time necessary to take care of a pet? Are you prepared for the disruption in routine and overall mess?

This includes basic needs such as feeding, walking and cleaning up after a dog, cleaning the litterbox, as well as socialization, training and companionship. Not only will you need to puppy- or kitten-proof the house, a litterbox and scratching post or dog toys and bones will also change the look of your home. Both cats and dogs can damage furniture or break fragile, decorative items on display. Dogs left outside without supervision can "re-landscape" by digging; dogs left inside uncrated and alone can "re-decorate" and destroy your home. A barking dog may upset or alienate your neighbors.

3. How many hours do you spend home per day? Do you work far away from the home or travel often?

Kittens and puppies should not be left alone for more than four hours at a time; adolescent (six months or older) to adult dogs should not be expected to "hold it" for over nine to ten hours. You will need to board your dog or hire a pet sitter while you are away for extended periods of time.

4. Do you have children or live in a neighborhood with children?

Children must be taught to play gently and to handle a cat or dog properly before bringing a pet into the home. Very young children are often too rough with kittens or puppies and can either get hurt or injure the pet. If adopting an older pet, make sure the cat or dog is used to children.

5. Do you have other pets? If so, can your household adapt easily to an additional pet?

Depending on individual personality traits, some pets will adapt more easily to new animals than others. Cats that have been exposed to dogs early in life–and vice versa–will likely be more accepting of them in their home (or new home, if adopted as adults). Multiple crates and bedding also take up more space.

6. Can you afford a pet … or another pet? What will happen to the pet if you become unable to care for it, either physically or financially?

Healthy cats' and dogs' lives can span nine to twenty years. That means many years' worth of food, grooming and veterinarian bills (including routine, neuter/spay and emergency). Add to that the additional costs of scratching posts, toys, bedding, crates or carriers, basic grooming tools, litterboxes and litter for cats, or replacement collars and leashes for dogs.

7. Is anyone in your household allergic to cats or dogs? Would the grooming needs of a longhaired or shorthaired breed suit you best?

Although some dog breeds do not shed or only shed seasonally, most dogs and cats shed daily. Some coats need to be brushed daily (such as Persians), trimmed and clipped every four to six weeks (such as Poodles) or have dead undercoat stripped out twice a year (most terriers).

8. Do you like the look of a specific breed or type? Do you prefer a specific size or activity level?

Kittens and puppies may start out small, but they won't stay that way if they are one of the larger or giant breeds! Many dogs, such as Border Collies, need mental stimulation, as well as a job to do, while a delicate toy breed, such as an Italian Greyhound, might not hold up to the rough play of a house full of young children. Dogs with oily coats (primarily water dogs) can retain unpleasant "doggy" odors. Dogs that were bred to work long, strenuous days hunting or in the fields are rarely content with minimal physical exercise, and often follow their instincts and noses. White cats with blue eyes, as well as certain dog breeds with this color combination, carry a high probability for deafness. When choosing a white coat color, check for deafness first.

Initial choices when looking for a pet:
- Cat or dog
- Male or female
- Kitten/puppy or cat/dog
- Longhaired or shorthaired
- Purebred or mix

Secondary choices:
- Size
- Appearance
- Color
- Spay/neuter
- Vocalization tendencies
- Ease of training
- Activity level
- Specific traits (herding tendencies, mouthiness, protective, good with children, etc.)
- Potential health problems common to the breed or type
- Grooming needs

Breed Types

Read books on cat or dog breeds, behavior and training; speak to local veterinarians; visit cat or dog shows and speak with breeders to become more familiar with the special traits of specific breeds or types of dogs or cats to which you are drawn. All-breed dog or cat shows offer the opportunity to speak with several breeders at once, and view many different breeds. Visiting a "specialty" dog breed show, where dozens of one specific breed are exhibited, will give you a twenty-four-hour-a-day, seven-day-a-week simulation of living with that breed. If you mind having the constantly wagging tails of a dozen Flat-coated Retrievers hitting your leg during an hour visit at a specialty show, chances are you will find that to be an annoying trait to live with for ten to fifteen years. Conversely, if you feel in heaven surrounded by dozens of these handsome, intelligent dogs, this may indeed be a good match.

Cats

More active and vocal cat breeds include Siamese, Abyssinian, Burmese, Balinese, Oriental Shorthair, Tonkinese, Cornish and Devon Rexes, Somali, Sphynx and Egyptian Mau. These breeds are not only active, but want to play all the time, including when you want to sleep. Also, Siamese, Burmese and Persians are typically more sociable and dependent upon human companionship, while the American Shorthair, Maine Coon and Manx are more independent.

Most cats weigh between eight and twelve pounds, but some of the larger breeds can weigh between fifteen and twenty pounds. Larger breeds include the Maine Coon, Norwegian Forest Cat, Ragdoll, Birman, Persian, Turkish Van, American Bobtail, British Shorthair, American Shorthair and the Chartreux. These larger cats are generally more easy-going, laid back, and tend to be quieter.

Non-pedigreed cats can have many of the traits above and make wonderful pets if chosen properly to mesh with your household. The domestic longhair or shorthair, often called the "alley cat," is the most common breed found in most pet homes. They are less expensive, easier to find, and come in a large variety of coat colors, lengths, body sizes, and temperaments.

Dogs

Many people prefer purebred dogs because of the predictability in character traits, looks, and size. Others prefer mixed breeds. Full-grown dogs can weigh anywhere from a 5-pound Chihuahua to a 185-pound Mastiff. The choices can be overwhelming, especially for a first-time dog owner.

Doing your research before bringing a puppy or adult dog home can help in preventing obviously wrong choices. For example, an active working dog, such as an Australian Shepherd or Bearded Collie can prove disastrous for a more sedentary person or a family with small children. Large, wet-mouthed dogs such as the Newfoundland would be a definite mismatch for anyone who prefers a clean home and clothes without drool spots. Certain breeds, such as the Bichon Frise or Basset Hound, can be difficult to housebreak; others, such as the Labrador Retriever, shed continuously. Many genetic diseases or problems are more prevalent in certain specific breeds or types. Some of the more popular breeds, including the German Shepherd or Golden Retriever, are genetically at higher risk to develop hip dysplasia, a progressive, degenerative joint disease.

This terrier goes everywhere with her owner, including out in the fields to chase away vermin. (Photo permission In Focus Imagery, Jeff Green)

A Puppy or Kitten?

Advantages:

❖ They're cute and playful.

❖ They can be taught the rules (right or wrong behavior) instead of having to re-direct bad habits already established. Teaches responsibility for older children.
It's easier to crate-train a puppy or to train or teach a kitten to use a scratching post.

❖ It's easier to get a puppy or kitten used to being handled by children, or being bathed and groomed.

Disadvantages:

❖ They're very time-consuming ... and a lot of work!

❖ They will need housebreaking and litterbox training. There will be lots of messes and accidents to clean up.

❖ You'll need to kitten- or puppy-proof your home.

❖ There will be more frequent feedings and veterinarian trips.

Both kittens and puppies need to be socialized with littermates and should not come home with their new family until seven to eight weeks old for puppies and thirteen weeks for kittens. (Photo courtesy Beth Ann Hill)

Adult Cat or Dog?

Advantages:

❖ There are no hidden surprises in temperament, size, coat, etc.

❖ Less time is needed for feeding, walks, etc.

❖ You'll have less work if the animal is already housebroken and obedience trained.

Disadvantages:

❖ An adult may have already established bad habits.

❖ Adults pets may not get along with or be accepted by other pets in household.

There is nothing more appealing than a baby cat or dog! They are so cute and cuddly and their antics so endearing, it is no wonder that most people fall in love with them. For many people, adopting an adult animal is sometimes more practical or preferable, whether due to lifestyle, time restraints or just the desire to avoid the work involved in housebreaking a pet. (Photo above by Linda Ziegler, photo bottom right, permission Barb Zurawski)

Finding Your Pet

Your goal should be to obtain a healthy, active, temperamentally sound cat or kitten, puppy or dog, with a good start in life. Your chances of getting a healthy, well-socialized animal, however, will increase if you take the time and energy to seek out reputable breeders, shelters or rescue groups. Anyone who has a litter of kittens or puppies can call themselves breeders. The difference is great between a reputable breeder, however, and someone whose motivations for breeding are for material gain. Sadly, each year millions of dogs and cats are euthanized, the end result of unwanted pets from irresponsible pet owners and breeders.

Breeders

CFA (Cat Fanciers Association), TICA (The International Cat Association), AKC (American Kennel Club) and UKC (United Kennel Club) are some of the official organizations for the purpose of registering purebred litters of dogs or cats. However, not all animals that have "papers" are from reputable breeders, and not all people calling themselves breeders register their litters. Whether a dog or cat is registered doesn't tell you about how it was raised, the health or temperament background of its parents or grandparents or how many litters per year its mother has produced. Responsible, reputable breeders rarely, if ever, make any money on the litters they raise and sell. It is most often the puppy and kitten mills, brokers and less-than-reputable breeders that sell animals as a "cash crop."

Good questions to ask a breeder:

❧ How long have you been breeding?

❧ How many different breeds do you handle?

❧ How many litters do you breed per year?

❧ What can you tell me about the breed?

❧ Do you show or do you belong to a breed club?

❧ Are there any hereditary diseases associated with this breed? If so, have both parents, as well as the grandparents, been screened and cleared? Has the litter been checked for deafness?

❧ Are the parents (or grandparents, half-littermates) on the premises?

❧ Do you provide a contract? Does it contain spay/neuter requirements or co-ownership restrictions? What health guarantees do you offer?

❧ Can you provide names and phone numbers of individuals who own dogs or cats from previous litters?

Reputable breeders devote much time, expense and care in breeding litters of only one or possibly two breeds. Their primary goal is to maintain high standards and improve the breed. Their commitment to their puppies or kittens continues even after the sale, with health guarantees, spay/neuter contracts, and the specification that the animal will be returned if the owner can no longer care for it. Many breeders have waiting lists for their puppies or kittens and take deposits on litters before the breeding even takes place.

Hobby breeders are often under the guidance of an experienced, reputable breeder or have been involved with dogs or cats and active in club or performance events for a number of years. They usually have only occasional litters and do not breed multiple breeds.

A reputable breeder will have bred more than one litter and should not have several litters to choose from with more on the way. A reputable breeder should not merely refer to the litter's pedigree being "from championship lines" without having had some personal involvement in showing over the years. A responsible breeder is concerned about passing on genetic diseases and will have had the

(Photo courtesy Linda Ziegler)

necessary screening and tests done on at least both parents. These can include specific problems inherent in the breed, as well as checking for more common problems, such as hip displaysia, heart, ear or eye problems. Ask to see a copy of these clearances, as well as the pedigree. Since a reputable breeder cares about the welfare of each puppy or kitten that they place, they will screen potential buyers and ask as many, if not more, questions of potential buyers than you might ask them. They will offer a health guarantee, be willing to give you references of other people who have purchased dogs or cats from previous litters, run a clean facility, and have a wealth of information about the breed.

Advantages to buying from a breeder

❧ You'll often receive a healthy, well-socialized breed with a good start in life.

❧ The breeder includes a health guarantee and contract.

❧ You can often see both parents and a written pedigree, going back several generations.

Disadvantages:

❧ It can take a lot of work and time to find a reputable breeder.

❧ Not all breeders will sell to your particular household or circumstances.

❧ Purebreds may be more expensive.

❧ Breeders might not have litters available when you are ready for a pet.

Reputable breeders can be found by contacting national or local breed clubs through various registries (see listing in Resource section on page 112). Since most reputable breeders are actively participating in some form of club membership activity, many can also be found at dog or cat shows. Other sources for finding reputable breeders include veterinarian recommendations, training facilities and referrals by others who have gotten healthy, temperamentally sound dogs or cats from a breeder.

Pet Stores and Backyard Breeders

"Back yard" breeders do so out of curiosity, for their children's experience, through accidental pregnancies of unspayed females, or with the idea of making some extra money. They may mean well, but are usually not knowledgeable enough about genetics and proper puppy/kitten socialization to be considered reputable breeders. Many of these litters are never officially registered, since it costs breeders to do so. These breeders generally place ads in newspapers, signs in front of their houses, or leave entire litters at an animal shelter.

The quality of socialization a puppy or kitten gets in a pet store will vary, depending on whether the animal was separated from its mother and littermates too soon, is kept in a cage by itself, or is susceptible to people poking at it. These early experiences, along with the inability to become familiar with the sights and sounds of a home environment and positive human interaction, can hamper this animal's start in life. The beginnings of housebreaking or litter training will be non-existent. Often puppies wind up being in this environment so long that they actually learn to eliminate in their cages, since they have no other option. This behavior can be very difficult, and sometimes impossible, to retrain. Kittens taken away from their mothers too soon can also have difficulty learning to use a litterbox.

Puppy and kitten mills sell puppies and kittens primarily via brokers and pet stores, but also through newspaper ads and the Internet. The horrors of these businesses have been written about in television, magazine, and newspaper exposés across the country. Multiple dogs or cats are kept in dirty, dark, crowded conditions and are bred each breeding season (twice a year or more). These litters are not socialized nor do the kittens and puppies have the proper positive contact with humans. They are often underfed and sick. Unfortunately, these businesses continue to exist because the demand for impulse purchases of puppies and kittens continues to exist.

All of these sources carry many unknowns. Interestingly, the price of puppies or kittens through a pet store, newspaper ad or puppy mill is often the same price asked by a more reputable breeder. Sometimes, even the "papers" that buyers are promised are either falsified or worthless, and do not come from an actual registry.

Advantages to buying from a pet store

● It's convenient and instantly gratifying for impulse buyers. There are many puppies and kittens to choose from.

● You can often find animals with mutated or unusual physical characteristics for the breed.

● No questions usually are asked nor is there groundwork to be done.

Disadvantages:

● All of the above.

Animal Shelters

Each year, eight million to twelve million animals enter shelters for various reasons, from unplanned litters to allergic owners to the new pet exhibiting adolescent behavior or bad habits. Others are abused, abandoned or found as strays. Good dogs and cats can be found in any shelter. You increase your chances, however, of finding a healthy, less stressed pet at shelters that are clean and have caring people working or volunteering there. The animals should appear healthy, have access to clean water and fresh air, and not have coughs or other signs of illness.

Advantages to adopting a pet from a shelter:

● You literally can save a dog's or cat's life.

● Some of the puppy and adolescent behavior can be avoided by adopting an adult, which may already be neutered or spayed.

● The physical appearance and size of adults are established, as is their temperament.

Disadvantages:

● You can wind up with a pet that has behavioral or physical problems that you did not expect or desire.

Although it might take a little longer for a rescue to bond, their love and appreciation from being rescued from the stress of a shelter and abandonment often reach a special level, especially when given a loving home. (Photo courtesy Sue Olmos)

Breed or Rescue Groups

These groups are generally made up of volunteers, most of whom sincerely love and are very knowledgeable about the idiosyncrasies of a specific breed. Many animals placed in rescue are there for the same reasons as animals in shelters. Often, they are placed in breed rescue because they haven't met the owner's expectations, or were recognized by a shelter as a purebred and placed in rescue. Potential owners are screened very thoroughly and may be turned down if they are considered unsuitable for a particular breed. The goal of placing a rescue animal in a home is to make a good match so the animal won't be returned to rescue to go through the trauma all over again. Sometimes, reputable breeders will also place adult dogs or cats, including animals returned because of an owner's ill health, as well as retired champions or older puppies not being suitable for their breeding program. Almost every recognizable breed has at least one rescue group, which can be found through national or regional breed clubs.

Advantages to rescuing a pet:

● The advantages are the same as for a shelter, plus it can be a wonderful opportunity to own a retired champion-quality animal.

● Many rescues already have had basic training.

Disadvantages:

● Rescue animals may be a great distance away and prove an unsuitable match only after making the trip.

● The screening process is often very strict.

● You may have to wait until a suitable animal is available.

I had lost my best friend of 20 years to cancer about six weeks before I met Zane Grey. I was very depressed when two friends came over to take me to a cat show to cheer me up. There was a woman at the show who does rescues … you often see wonderful booths like this at local cat shows. She had cages stacked way, way up, with all kinds of beautiful rescued kitties that needed homes. As I stood in front of the cages, just looking with wonder at all of those little faces, Zane stuck his paw out of his cage, as if to say "Hey, look over here, here I am!" I looked into his eyes and felt my heart stir. There he was, just a plain gray kitty, about seven months old, peering into my eyes with his paw extended out to me. I don't know what it was, but he really seemed to like me. I walked over to him and took his little paw in my hand and started crying. Even my friends remarked how special it appeared to them, how he had just picked me out. Well, I took him home that day. He sat on my lap in the back seat of the car, never moving an inch, as if he somehow knew he was "home."

(Photo permission Barb Zurawski/Beth Ann Hill)

Zane has since won many hearts, earning the honored Second Best Household Pet (HHP) title at the International Cat Association (TICA) regional show and the Seventh Best HHP title internationally in 1999. He has been there through my joys and sorrows, has dried many a tear and given me many kisses. Zane is my dearest friend, my forever friend.

-Beth Ann Hill

Spay/Neuter

Experts agree that neutering a cat or dog is a key to making most animals a better pet. In addition to avoiding unpleasant marking and seasonal bleeding, it can also help curb aggressiveness and some adolescent behaviors. The act of mating itself can involve high physical risks for male dogs. Complications, often fatal, can occur for female dogs or cats during pregnancy and/or birth.

Advantages to spaying and neutering your pet:

🐾 Neutered males are not as apt to mark territory. Spayed females do not go into "season" and bleed.

🐾 It can prevent or greatly reduce aggressive behavior and reduces the tendency to vocalize, escape, or roam in both males and females.

🐾 It eliminates weeks of sleepless nights, hard work, and expense of unwanted litters of a dozen or more puppies or kittens.

🐾 It reduces risk of prostate cancer in males, eliminates risk of uterine cancer in females.

Disadvantage:

🐾 Your pet cannot have litters of puppies or kittens.

A pet can become a valuable and beloved member of your household, if given the time and care it needs. Although you must be willing and able to invest money in your new pet's routine and emergency vet care, proper nutrition and grooming, a puppy or kitten should never be thought of as an acquisition or a financial investment, like a house or car. Neither should a pet be thought of as an amusement that can just be sold or discarded if its owners lose interest.

Chapter 2
REST YOUR PAWS

Before You Bring Home a Puppy or Kitten

Kittens climb; puppies chew. All healthy kittens and puppies are curious about their environment and will begin to explore it the first day you bring your new pet home. Think beyond child proofing; think like a puppy or kitten. Imagine a cat or a dog as a perpetual two-year-old and remove items that you would not leave out for a toddler to play with or ingest. Scrutinize your home from their perspective: are electric or phone cords dangling at floor level begging to be chewed on, poisonous plants accessible to nibble on, small children's toys and other objects left strewn about? String, ribbon, yarn, and other similar materials should be safely put away to prevent curious kittens or puppies from swallowing them. Window blinds or drapery cords pose dangers as do open wastebaskets and garbage cans.

Make sure all cleaning chemicals, medicines, cosmetics, or other potential poisons are safely locked away. Keep drawers shut, cabinet doors closed, and even locked with safety locks to prevent curious kittens and puppies from exploring their contents. Keep toilet lids down and make sure to rinse all floors, showers, bathtubs and sinks that your pet will have access to, especially after cleaning them. Change to environmentally safe, non-toxic cleaning products, such as vinegar and water for floors and mirrors. Make sure all pesticides, fertilizers, chemical salts, and antifreeze are cleaned up—even better, change to non-toxic, organic lawn and garden care. However, dogs can still pick up these chemicals from the neighbors' lawns or sidewalks and then ingest them when they lick their paws. Wipe or rinse your pet's feet off after a walk to reduce the potential hazard.

Kittens and larger puppies can easily learn to steal food from tables and counters; remove this temptation by putting away all food. Make sure your window and door screens are securely attached, especially on upper story windows. Some foods, like chocolate and onions (cooked or raw), are toxic to dogs and cats. If ingested in large enough quantities proportionate to their size, these foods can even be fatal. (If you wish to treat your dog or cat, try offering carob-based treats; they're a safe and natural alternative to real chocolate treats.)

Kittens' and puppies' training needs are different. Kittens need to be trained to use a litterbox, a scratching post instead of furniture, and to climb on a cat tree instead of your draperies or counters. Puppies need to be housebroken, leash trained, learn basic obedience commands (see p. 86), and taught what is and is not appropriate to chew. All these can be better learned when your puppy or kitten isn't allowed to roam freely throughout the house.

Providing a crate or carrier for your pet for rides in the car, especially your initial trip home, will be one of the best safety investments you will ever make. Crate-training a dog at home also has distinct advantages, including as an aid in housebreaking and providing your pet with a "safe" place all his own. (Photo courtesy Jeff and Lea Harris)

It is best to confine your kitten or puppy in one small room or gated-off area that is totally puppy- or kitten-proofed for the first few weeks. This will aid greatly in housebreaking and litter training, as well as provide a safer environment. However, this does not mean that you should just lock your new baby away in a bathroom or leave it alone in the kitchen unsupervised. Your new pet will need to be with you much of the time. Plan to do more of your activities in the room or area that you have puppy- or kitten-proofed, so that you and your new family member can properly bond.

Make sure that you use child-approved safety gates that cannot fall on a rambunctious puppy or climbing kitten. Providing a crate or carrier for your puppy or kitten when you cannot supervise them will not only aid in housebreaking, but will also cut down on destructive chewing, digging, and climbing. Dogs instinctively will not want to eliminate in what they perceive to be their "den." By confining a puppy to one room (or portion of a room) that she perceives as her "den," and bringing her outside to eliminate, that instinct will be doubly reinforced. Otherwise, the puppy might think of the room that her bed or crate is in as the den and the living room or upstairs bedroom as "outside the den" and a good spot to "go" in.

Teach your puppy or kitten to associate being in the crate or carrier with pleasure. Throw a treat or toy in the crate or carrier and encourage your pet to go inside to retrieve it. First get him used to just going in and out, praising him each time he goes in. Use a positive tone of voice and a command word or phrase ("Go to your room" or "Crate") to help him associate the crate with the command. Put your pet in the crate for short periods of time–even for just a few minutes–when you are in the same room. Then let him out. Gradually increase the time he spends in his crate and the distance you are from the crate, until you can leave the room for a few minutes and then return without him barking or whining.

Never use an angry tone of voice for the command to go there so he will get used to the idea of being in the crate as a place of his own, instead of as a punishment or as isolation. Having "time out" in a crate will also help him to associate being in a crate with a feeling of safety during stressful times, such as thunderstorms, or to escape household upsets. It is also a good aid to prevent separation anxiety or for when unsafe household conditions exist, such as repairs or remodeling.

Positive Reinforcement
Associating an act or behavior with pleasant sensations such as verbal praise, a treat or playing is referred to as positive reinforcement.

Escaping
One way to prevent your puppy or kitten from getting the idea that he can run out the front door is to get him to associate the front door with *entering* rather than exiting the house. If possible, avoid taking a puppy out of the house via the front door until he is over one year old or is reliably obedience trained. Exit the house through a back or side door, one that hopefully leads to a fenced-in back yard, dog run, or other enclosed area. Always take the dog out on a leash. At the same time, teach a dog to sit at the front door whenever family members or guests enter and exit the house. Keep a leash near the front door and, when the doorbell rings, clip it on the dog, tell him to sit and *then* open the door. Praise the puppy for sitting and give him a treat. Soon the puppy will associate sitting at the front door as something wonderful to do. Do the same thing when someone is exiting. When you are too busy to work with training, place a child's safety gate in the hallway or kitchen, and keep the puppy confined to one area (or crated) when the children are home and running in and out of the house.

Things you will need when you bring your pet home:	
Cat or Kitten	**Dog or Puppy**
Food: Ask veterinarian or breeder for advice	Same
Two bowls: one for food, one for water	Same
Soft, quick-release cat collar with an ID tag	Leather, or nylon buckle or clip dog collar with ID tag
Litterbox, litter, scoop, and optional mat	Leash, plastic bags, scoop/bucket to dispose of feces
Scratching post	Rawhide or rubber chew toys
Nail trimmer and styptic powder	Same
Enzyme odor cleaner	Same
Cat toys	Dog toys
Brush and/or comb	Same
Toothbrush and enzyme based toothpaste	Same
Travel crate	Same, plus crate for inside the home
Child-safe gates	Same

Sleeping Habits

Cats and dogs sleep more than humans—up to eighteen hours per day. Both cats and dogs can make a nuisance of themselves, however, when they get into the habit of early morning or nighttime waking. To prevent this behavior from forming, try playing with them more during the day and keeping them awake later in the evening. A cat or a dog that sleeps all evening (as well as most of the day) will be wide-awake early in the morning or during the night. Go for an evening walk, play a brisk game of catch, go to a training class, or simply play in the house with your pet. You will both sleep better!

Dogs who aren't crated, or in a gated room, can wake you up early if they want their breakfast or need to go to the bathroom. Limiting or preventing water intake beyond the early evening, especially for puppies, will help stretch out the need for bathroom trips during the night. If your dog wakes you early, do not respond by giving her breakfast. Instead, take her out to do her business (without any socialization or playing) and return her to her sleeping area. If the dog insists on following you back to your bed, you may want to consider crate-training your dog. Use a water mister if your cat pesters you, instead of responding by getting out of bed. Since it is possible that your dog or cat really is very hungry, try feeding the last meal later in the evening or offer your dog a bedtime treat, such as a dog biscuit, before bed.

Sleeping Tips

🐾 Since cats feel naturally drowsy after a meal, feed your cat just before your bedtime.

🐾 Playing with your pet will tire her out enough to sleep.

🐾 Keep your pet in a separate room or crated at night; do not allow your pet in your bed, unless you want her there every night for her entire life.

3/4 yard each of 2 contrasting or coordinating 44/45"
width fabric prints (mattress and pillow)
1-3/4 yards of coordinating fabric (bed frame)
1 large bag of polyester fiberfill
Heavyweight polyester quilt-batting (baby-quilt size)
Cotton batting (baby-quilt size)
2 clean, grocery-size paper bags (see page 6)
Yardstick, pencil, scissors, straight pins or quilting pins
Matching thread
4 yards of 3/8" ribbon or 7/8" wide single fold bias tape
Optional: 2 tassels

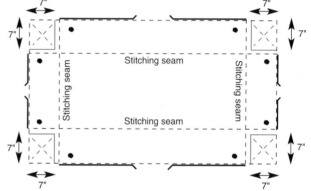

Diagram

Legend for diagram:
- - - - - - - - Side seam guidelines (black)
- - - - - - - - Seam allowance (orange)
⌐   ⌐ Leave open
•   Insert ribbon or seam tape
——— Pattern line

Bed frame:

1. Create pattern: Cut out two 15" x 33" rectangles
using materials listed above and tape together along one
33" edge, overlapping 1" to secure. This will create a
29" x 33" rectangle.

2. Per Diagram, draw side-seam guidelines 7" from
each edge. Mark an "X" in each corner.

3. Mark seam allowance by drawing lines 6-1/2" from
each edge. Cut out the 6-1/2" square corners created
in this step.

4. Using the pattern created in Steps 1-3, cut out 2
pieces of fabric and one piece of each type of batting. Place the 2 fabric pieces RST over the 2 batting
pieces, matching edges very carefully. Pin in place along the outer edges, leaving a 5" section open in the
center of each of the long outer edges, as per Diagram.

5. Cut the ribbon or bias tape into eight 18" lengths. (Note: If using bias tape, fold each 18" length in half
and stitch together, tucking in one short end on each length.) Insert the ribbon or tape into each short
seam, just beneath the top layer of fabric, with the non-tucked short end lined up at the stitching line, 2"
from the long edge; see Diagram.

6. Make sure the ribbon or tape is carefully tucked inside the fabric layers and away from all seam edges.
Straight stitch through all 4 layers 1/2" from the edge along the stitching seam, leaving the 5" sections
open, as indicated in Step 4. Reinforce the stitching along the stitching seam in the inside corners and
where the ribbon/tape was inserted.

Paws-itively The Best Pet Bed
Cut 2 contrasting rectangular pieces of Berber fleece, fake fur or other heavy-duty fabric (27" x 35", 32" x 42", 38" x 50"). Appliqué contrasting fabric in your choice of image, using enlarged templates on pages 109-111). Allowing a 1" seam allowance, stitch around the edges, adding a (12", 14", 16") strip of hook and loop tape along one open edge. Stuff with a pre-made pillow insert, or make your own. Finished sizes: (S) 25" x 33", (M) 30" x 40", (L) 36" x 48".

7. Turn RSO through one of the 5" openings. Lay flat. Using a yardstick for a guide, measure and pin a line along the side seam guideline that was drawn in Step 2. (Tip: Place the yardstick from one inside corner across to the other.) Stitch along the pinned line.

8. Tie the sides together. Lightly stuff each side section. Hand-sew the openings shut. (Optional: Topstitch all along the outer edges, 3/8" from each edge and retie.)

Mattress:
1. Cut out two 18" x 22" pieces from contrasting fabric for the mattress. Sew along the edges, RST, leaving a 6" opening. Turn RSO.

2. Lightly stuff with fiberfill. Hand-sew the opening shut.

Pillow:
1. Cut out one 12" x 19" piece of fabric for the pillow. Fold and press each short edge under 1". Fold the fabric in half lengthwise, RST. Stitch along the long edge. Turn RSO.

2. Sew a running or gathering stitch along the short edge, 1/2" from the edge, stitching through both layers of fabric plus the pressed under edges. Turn RSO.

3. Pull threads to gather on one end and tie securely. Trim thread ends. Stuff the pillow with fiberfill. Gather and tie the remaining end, trimming threads. Hand-tack the tassels to the short ends of the pillow.

Creative Options:

• Add a ruffle, fringe or other trim onto the edge of the bed frame.

• Hand or machine embroider or monogram your pet's initials onto the pillow or mattress before stuffing.

• Using embroidery floss, hand-stitch a decorative stitch, such as a blanket or overcast stitch, around the edges of the bed frame.

Berber fleece, fake fur, or other suitable heavy-duty fabric (See chart below for yardage)
Fiberfill
Straight pins
Pencil
Thread
2 clean, grocery size paper bags (see page 6)

Yardage Chart:
Small cat or small dog:
15"+ 36" circles   (1-1/2 yards of fabric 36" wide or wider)
Medium/large:
20" + 48" circles (2 yards of fabric 48" wide or wider)
X-large:
25" + 60" circles (2-1/2 yards of fabric 60" wide or wider)

Sizes:
1. Create two circle patterns in the appropriate sizes (above) and cut out one of each size from the fabric. Fold the small and large circles in quarters and mark each fold along the outer edge with a pin.

2. Hand or machine stitch 2 rows of gathering stitches around the edges of the larger circle, 1/4" and 1/2" from the outer edge, beginning and ending in the quarter round sections, as marked. Pull each section of the larger circle to gather, tying off one end in each section to prevent the thread from slipping out.

3. Place the smaller circle in the center of the larger one, RST. Place the edges of the smaller circle against the large gathered edge, RST and matching pins from Step 2. Pin together, adjusting gathering one section at a time if necessary.

4. Stitch in place, 3/8" from outer edge, leaving a 6" opening to turn. Stitch a second time to reinforce the seams. Turn RST and stuff with fiberfill. Hand-sew shut. Push down in the center to form the nest shape.

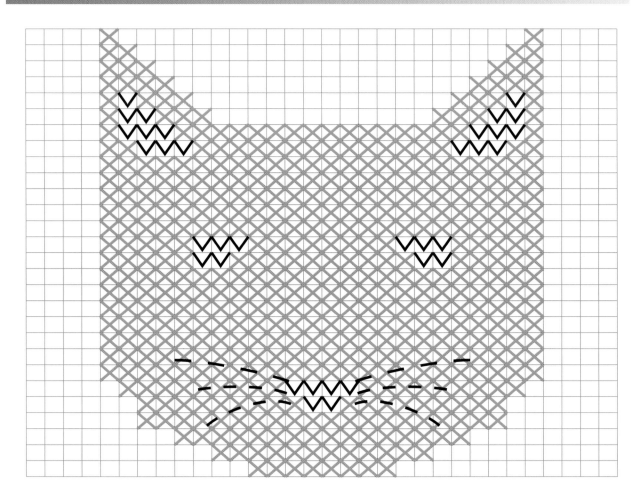

by Lee Danenberg

MC= Main Color
Stockinette stitch is knit one row, purl one row.
Garter stitch is knit one row, knit one row.
Gauge: 24 sts and 32 rows in stockinette stitch on size 4 needles
2 oz. worsted yarn in MC (Kitten—Rose Heather 140; Puppy—Butterscotch 189)*
1 oz. worsted yarn in color A (Kitten—Dark Rose Heather 139, Puppy—Copper 190)*
1/2 oz. worsted yarn in color B (Kitten—White Multi-Color 301, Puppy—Espresso 128)*
Small amount of worsted yarn in color C (Kitten—Denim 114, Puppy—Black 153, Ranch Red 102)*
1 pair each size (small: #2 and #4; medium: #3 and #5; large: #4 and #6) knitting needles
Yarn needle
Yarn bobbins (kitten: 2 for hat, 2 for scarf; puppy: 4 for hat, 5 for scarf)
Crochet hook

* All yarn used is Wool-Ease, Lion Brand Yarn

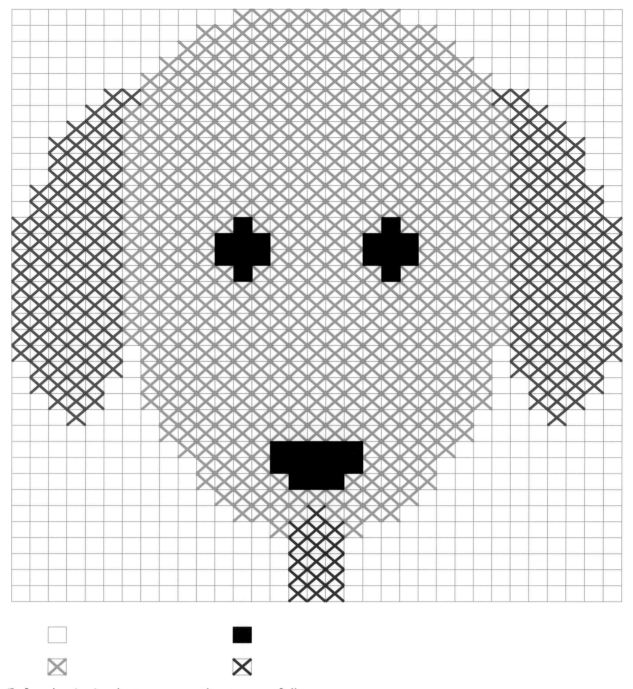

Before beginning hat, prepare the yarn as follows:
• Kitten: Divide the 2 oz. ball of MC into 2 equal smaller balls. Wind some of the MC onto one yarn bobbin and color B onto another bobbin. Set aside.

• Puppy: Wind small amounts of color B and black each on 2 bobbins. Set aside.

Before beginning scarf, prepare the yarn as follows:
• Kitten: Wind some of the MC and color B each onto separate bobbins

• Puppy: Divide the 2 oz. ball of MC into 2 equal smaller balls. Wind color B and small amounts of black each onto separate yarn bobbins; wind a small amount of red onto 1 yarn bobbin. Set aside.

• Twist yarns firmly together when changing colors to avoid making holes.

• Amount of yarn listed is for each knitted item

• For scarf pockets: If desired, knit both pockets at the same time, using two separate balls of MC

1. Using smaller needles and Color A, cast on 112 stitches. Work in K1, P1 rib for 4 inches. Puppy hat only: Increase 1 stitch in the last row.

2. Change to larger needles and the first small ball of MC. Work 8 rows in a stockinette stitch, beginning with a K row and ending with a P row.

Work the kitten design as follows:
Row 1: K52 MC, K8 B (Attach second ball of MC), K52 MC
Row 2: P50 MC, P12 B, P50 MC
Row 3: K48 MC, K16 B, K48 MC
Row 4: P46 MC, P20 B, P46 MC
Row 5: K46 MC, K20 B, K46 MC
Row 6: P45 MC, P22 B, P45 MC
Rows 7-22: K1 row, P 1 row as follows:
        K44 MC, K24 B, K44 MC
        P44 MC, P24 B, P44 MC
Row 23: K44 MC, K6 B (Attach bobbin of MC), K12 MC, K6 B, K44 MC
Row 24: P44 MC, P5 B, P14 MC, P5 B, P44 MC
Row 25: K44 MC, K4 B, K16 MC, K4 B, K44 MC
Row 26: P44 MC, P3 B, P18 MC, P3 B, P44 MC
Row 27: K44 MC, K2 B, K20 MC, K2 B, K44 MC
Row 28: P44 MC, P1 B, P22 MC, P1 B, P44 MC

Work the puppy design as follows:

Row 1: K55 MC, K3 Red, attach second ball of MC,
    K55 MC
Row 2: P55 MC, P3 Red, P55 MC
Row 3: K55 MC, K3 Red, K55 MC
Row 4: P55 MC, P3 Red, P55 MC
Row 5: K54 MC, K1 A, K3 Red, K1 A, K54 MC
Row 6: P52 MC, P4 A, P1 Red, P4 A, P52 MC
Row 7: K51 MC, K11 A, K51 MC
Row 8: P50 MC, P5 A, P3 Black, P5 A, P50 MC
Row 9: K50 MC, K4 A, K5 Black, K4 A, K50 MC
Row 10: P49 MC, P5 A, P5 Black, P5 A, P49 MC
Row 11: K48 MC, K17 A, K48 MC
Row 12: P43 MC, P1 B, P4 MC, P17 A, P4 MC, P1 B,
        P43 MC
Row 13: K42 MC, K3 B, K2 MC, K19 A, K2 MC, K3 B,
        K42 MC
Row 14: P41 MC, P4 B, P2 MC, P19 A, P2 MC, P4 B,
        P41 MC
Row 15: K41 MC, K5 B, K1 MC, K19 A, K1 MC, K5 B,
        K41 MC
Row 16: P40 MC, P6 B, P21 A, P6 B, P40 MCRow 17:
        K40 MC, K6 B, K21 A, K6 B, K40 MC
Row 18: P40 MC, P6B, P21 A, P6 B, P40 MC
Rows 19 & 20: Repeat rows 17 & 18
Row 21: K40 MC, K6 B, K6 A, K1 Black, K7 A, K1
        Black, K6 A, K6 B, K40 MC
Row 22: P40 MC, P6 B, P5 A, P3 Black, P5 A, P3
        Black, P5 A, P6 B, P40 MC

Row 23: K40 MC, K6 B, K5 A, K3 Black, K5 A, K3
        Black, K5 A, K6 B, K40 MC
Row 24: P40 MC, P6 B, P6 A, P1 Black, P7 A, P1
        Black, P6 A, P6 B, P40 MC
Row 25: K41 MC, K5 B, K21 A, K5 B, K41 MC
Row 26: P41 MC, P5 B, P21 A, P5 B, P41 MC
Row 27: K42 MC, K4 B, K21 A, K4 B, K42 MC
Row 28: P42 MC, P4 B, P21 A, P4 B, P42 MC
Row 29: K42 MC, K4 B, K21 A, K4 B, K42 MC
Row 30: P43 MC, P3 B, P21 A, P3 B, P43 MC
Row 31: K44 MC, K2 B, K21 A, K2 B, K44 MC
Row 32: P45 MC, P2 B, P19 A, P2 B, P45 MC
Row 33: K47 MC, K19 A, K47 MC
Row 34: P48 MC, P17 A, P48 MC
Row 35: K49 MC, K15 A, K49 MC
Row 36: P50 MC, P13 A, P50 MC
Row 37: K52 MC, K9 A, K52 MC
Row 38: Purl across with MC

Continue in a stockinette stitch with the MC only, until the piece measures (kitten—10"; puppy—11") from the beginning. End with a purl row.

3. Last row: (For puppy only: Knit 2 together at beginning of this row so you have 112 stitches.) K1, K3 together, repeating this pattern to the end of the row. Leave at least 24" of yarn at the end of the row. Using a yarn needle, thread the yarn through the remaining stitches, taking the stitches off the knitting needle as you do so. Leave the remaining yarn end in reserve for Step 6. Carefully weave in all loose ends from creating the kitten or puppy face on the wrong side.

Finishing:

1. Kitten only: With the yarn needle and Color A, use Duplicate Stitch (see General Instructions, page 6) to fill in the kitten's nose and the center of each ear. Stitch the kitten's eyes with Color C. Backstitch the kitten's whiskers, using only 2 strands of Color C.

2. Carefully pull the reserved 24" length of yarn from Step 4 tightly together, joining it to the other end of the row to close the top of the hat. Tack a few stitches to secure. Using the remaining length of yarn, stitch the back of the hat together. When you reach the ribbing, switch colors to complete the seam. (Note: To stitch the back of the hat, weave the yarn along the edge of the knitting, alternating sides to make a smooth, almost seamless joining. Tack 2 or 3 times to end the stitching of each color.)

3. Make a 2"or larger pompom in color of your choice. Pull the ends of the pompom through to the wrong side of the top of the hat and stitch firmly in place.

Notes for duplicate stitch:
• Use heavy enough yarn to completely cover the knitted stitch.
• Duplicate stitch is most effective done over a stockinette stitch.
• Use a large, blunt needle and a short piece of yarn (1 yard maximum).
• When applying the stitches, work horizontally or diagonally.
• Avoid pulling the stitch too tightly.
• For a half-stitch, bring the needle and yarn to the WS instead of in front.

KITTEN SCARF

1. Using #6 needles and color B, cast on 8 stitches. Work 2 rows in stockinette stitch.

2. Work kitten design as follows, increasing on knit (odd) rows:

Row 1: Increase in first 2 stitches, K across to next to last 2 stitches. Increase in last 2 stitches (12 stitches)
Row 2: Purl across entire row.
Row 3: Continue increasing on each K row as in Row 1, until you have 28 stitches on the needle.
Rows 4-16: Continue with the stockinette stitch, for 16 rows, ending with a purl row.

Row 17: K8 B, K12 MC, K8 B	Row 22: P3 B, P22 MC, P3 B
Row 18: P7 B, P14 MC, P7 B	Row 23: K2 B, K24 MC, K2 B
Row 19: K6 B, K16 MC, K6 B	Row 24: P1 B, P26 MC, P1 B
Row 20: P5 B, P18 MC, P5 B	Rows 25- 32: With MC,
Row 21: K4 B, K20 MC, K4 B	K1 row, P1 row for 8 rows

Striped Pattern:
With Color A, K1 row, P1 row.
With Color B, K1 row, P1 row.
With Color A, K1 row, P1 row.
With MC, K1 row, P1 row for 16 rows.
Continue until the scarf measures approximately 40", ending with 9 rows of stockinette stitch in MC. (Note: The last row will be a K row.)

3. On the wrong side, weave in all the loose ends created by making the stripes.

4. Using color B, work the kitten in reverse, beginning with Row 24. Start to decrease in Row 9 by knitting 2 together at the beginning and end of each K row until 8 stitches remain. K1 row, P1 row; then cast off.

5. With the yarn needle and the following colors, use the duplicate stitch (see General Instructions on page 6) to add the kitten's features: Ears (MC), nose (A), eyes (C). Stitch the whiskers, using only 2 strands and a backstitch.

6. Make two pockets as follows:
For each pocket, cast on 8 stitches and work rows 1-3 as above. Continue in stockinette stitch until the piece measures 5". Using MC, K1, P1, in ribbing for 6 rows. Bind off.

Finishing:

1. With the WS together, sew one pocket to the WS of the kitten's head design at each end of the scarf, leaving the top edge open.

Optional: To minimize curling, single crochet 2 rows along each long edge of the scarf.

2. Block by wetting the finished piece. Lay out to dry on a flat surface.

Puppy Scarf

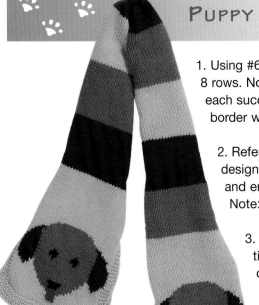

1. Using #6 needles and MC, cast on 41 stitches. Work in garter stitch for 8 rows. Note: Work 4 stitches in garter stitch at the beginning and end of each succeeding row for the full length of the scarf. All rows between this border will be in stockinette stitch. Work 4 rows in MC.

2. Referring to the graph, work the 33 stitches and 37 rows of puppy design, being sure to knit the rows of garter stitch at the beginning and end of each row.
Note: Odd numbers are K rows; even numbers are P rows.

3. Knit the scarf as long as you desire, changing colors and knitting alternating rows of stripes in color combinations of your choice. End with a P row.

4. Continue to work the garter stitch border. Working backwards on the puppy design graph, start with row 37 and knit the puppy design.

5. Starting with a P row, work 4 rows in stockinette stitch in MC.

6. Work in garter stitch for 8 rows. Cast off. Weave in all loose ends of yarn.

Pockets:

Cast on 41 stitches with MC. Work in garter stitch for 8 rows.

1. Working 4 stitches in garter stitch at both ends of each row, work in stockinette stitch until the piece measures 6" from the beginning, ending with a P row.

2. Decrease 1 stitch (K2 together) at the beginning of the next row. Work the remaining 40 stitches in ribbing for 4 rows. Cast off.

3. With the wrong sides together, and working on the RS, stitch the pockets to the scarf. Block.

Adding Another Pet

Introducing a second cat or dog demands patience and careful supervision. It can be easier if you introduce a kitten or puppy, and/or already have neutered or spayed animals currently in the home. Carefully observe and supervise all interactions in those important first weeks. Confine the new animal in a separate room or gated area for awhile and observe its reactions. Eventually, allow some short, supervised contact between the newcomer and your original pet(s). Use food treats and verbal praise to reward "nice" behavior, avoiding punishment for "bad" behavior so the ani-

Photo courtesy Jeff and Lea Harris

mals do not associate the negative experience with each other. Continue several short daily intervals, gradually feeding them in closer proximity to each other. Eventually, encourage them both to play with you. If you are introducing a cat into a dog household—or vice versa—make sure that the litterbox and the cat's food will not be accessible to the dog. If necessary, spend quality time alone with your original pet to make sure he doesn't feel replaced or ignored.

It is wise to introduce two adult dogs in a neutral territory, *away from the home*, using leash restraint until both dogs exhibit consistently friendly behavior. Make sure that the dogs are not left together, unsupervised, until you are positive that they get along. All cats have some territorial instincts and will think of the new animal as an intruder. Try to spend more time with both cats, since your presence may be comforting enough to reduce some of the stress.

Photo courtesy Dee Coleman

Fears

Changes in environment, as well as sound or sight sensitivity, can evoke fear in many pets. Puppies and kittens all go through "fear" stages, during which time they are more sensitive to having unusual or frightening experiences imprinted on them as fearful. Since cats and dogs do not deal with changes in environment as well as humans do, they need a period of adjustment when changes occur. Changes can be very stressful for your pet, whether they are simple ones, such as rearranging the furniture or getting new drapes, or more extreme changes such as moving to a new house or the arrival of a baby.

Both cats and dogs instinctively seek small, dark, den-like hiding places, especially when afraid or nervous (lots of noisy company or during a thunderstorm). For this reason, make sure that unsafe choices, such as open clothes dryers, aren't accessible. During a thunderstorm, some dogs will panic and run out of the house in terror if there are no secure spots in which they can hide. A cold and frightened cat will often creep up under the hood of a recently parked car near the still-warm engine, fall asleep, and then become trapped and injured when the unknowing motorist starts the car and begins to drive.

Rewarding calm or acceptable behavior often helps de-sensitize a dog or cat to frightening sounds like thunderstorms or fireworks. You might consider exposing the animal to taped sounds of storms or celebrations, gradually increasing the volume and duration as they gain tolerance. You should always act calm and relaxed yourself during frightening sounds. If the problem continues, talk to your veterinarian about anti-anxiety medications or holistic treatments.

Fear of strangers can be avoided by socializing your kitten or puppy when young. Positive experiences with many different types of people, including large, old, handicapped, other races, children, both women and men, and those wearing hats or beards, will help your pet become comfortable with meeting different people, no matter how they look.

Children and Pets

How to hold a kitten or puppy: place one hand on the chest, directly behind the front legs. Gently lift the rear end and hind legs with your other hand.

Dogs bite. So do cats—and they scratch as well. The keys to children and cats or dogs safely interacting include adult supervision and teaching children how to handle and play with their pets properly. Many of the dog and cat bites and clawing incidents treated each year are due to provocation, often in ignorance. Teach children how to hold a cat correctly, with support under her chest and without letting her legs dangle. They also should not pull toys or bones out of a dog's mouth or approach a dog frontally, staring into his eyes. Children sometimes run up behind dogs or cats to pet them, startling them unintentionally. Wild, threatening movements, even in play, may not be interpreted as playful by a pet that is not used to such activity. Such movements may instead trigger instinctive canine or feline play behavior, which can include biting, clawing, growling, or dominance posturing. Information on canine or feline behavior can be found at any library or bookstore, or on dozens of informational sites on the Internet. Knowing how dogs or cats think will help establish and maintain a mutual and loving bond between children and their pets.

Young, exuberant puppies become larger, stronger, exuberant adolescent puppies. If a child is young or not strong, a puppy on a leash will be able to pull free and escape. If chased, the fun of escaping becomes reinforced and turned into a game that your puppy will try to initiate over and over. An adult or older child should hold the leash in potentially excitable situations, until the puppy is better trained or the child is more confident or stronger. Attending obedience classes can teach adults and children, especially if they are new to dog ownership, better ways of controlling their pets.

Photo courtesy Pat Schulz and Maureen Tobias

Chapter 3
HOW CATS AND DOGS THINK

Differences or Similarities?

While the domestic dog has freely chosen man's hearth and has been a loyal, devoted companion and helper for centuries, a cat tends to choose human companionship on its own terms. As hunters in the wild, dogs are pack animals, viewing their human families as their "pack" with its natural hierarchy of social standing and leadership. Cats, on the other hand, are solitary hunters. In a domestic setting, however, cats can form a social structure of their own and bond strongly with their human companions and other household pets.

Hearing, balance, and vision are more acute in cats than their sense of smell, while dogs' senses of smell and hearing are more acute than their vision. Cats can see in dim light, have very strong depth perception, and can see color; dogs see moving objects best. Both cats and dogs can hear sounds at frequencies that humans cannot detect. This is what makes dogs good sentinels and aids cats in finding prey such as mice, which communicate in high-pitched sounds that are inaudible to us. A dog's hearing is so finely tuned, he is even capable of hearing and recognizing the approach of his owner's car from blocks away. As a rule, cats are more dexterous with their paws than dogs, but dogs are easier to train. By using some of the approaches that you would use to train a puppy, however, a cat can be taught basic commands. Cats and dogs also learn by observing other cats and dogs, as in litterbox use or sheep herding.

Both cats and dogs use body language to communicate. Cats rub against people to deposit scent, essentially marking the object as belonging to them, while dogs rub against people to reinforce the social bond. Dropping into a "play-bow" visually demonstrates a dog's desire to play. Submissive gestures, such as briefly looking away when a person or another dog approaches, or rolling on its back and exposing its stomach indi-cates a dog's acceptance of a person or another dog as being the leader. Other canine body language includes turning the head to one side when recognizing a spoken word, or licking a person or another canine's face as a friendly greeting. Dogs and cats exhibit very different body language when it comes to their tails. A tail carried high in a cat is a sign of contentment; in a dog it signals excitement or a warning of dominance or aggression. A dog's wagging tail is known to signal pleasure, but a cat's wagging tail is a warning. Purring is a sign of contentment, but exactly how a cat purrs is a scientific mystery.

Dogs and cats lick for different reasons. Cats lick their fur to groom and likewise lick their owners as if they were grooming them. Dogs, on the other hand, lick people to demonstrate affection or interest, the same way we use our hands to pet them. Dogs also lick us to signal they want something to eat or to reinforce their respect for our authority, just as they signaled their moms when puppies. Both cats and dogs will also lick themselves to reduce anxiety or stress. A stressed cat or dog can lick itself to the point of creating sores, which could require medical attention.

Like humans, individual temperaments in both cats and dogs vary, including being more or less active, playful, laid-back, vocal, friendlier, insecure, aggressive, or independent. Traits can be due partly to specific breeds, parents' temperaments or environmental situations. Although we humans can't always choose our relatives or their traits, we *can* choose our pets!

(Photo permission In Focus Imagery, Jeff Green)

Avoiding or Correcting Problem Behavior

It is easier to prevent bad behavior or habits from forming than to try to correct undesirable habits once they have formed. The longer the habit has existed, the more difficult it will be to change. If problem behaviors seem to be getting worse, or are causing serious problems or injury, contact an animal behavior specialist or veterinarian. Behavior specialists can help identify the causes of problem behavior and develop modification exercises to help you work through these problems. Sometimes there are physical reasons for certain behaviors, especially if they are sudden or unusual, which need to be treated by your veterinarian. *Above all, no matter how angry you are, never strike your cat or dog, except in extreme self-defense!* Physical abuse will only succeed in hurting your pet, make your dog or cat lose its trust in you, and encourage aggressiveness. Your pet will also associate the punishment with you, rather than with their undesirable behavior.

Train your pet using positive reinforcement for the correct behavior. *In other words, teach pets that actions have consequences.* When a dog or cat acts correctly, give it good things, such as praise, petting, food, toys, or playtime. These rewards help the animal associate her behavior with your response, and ultimately learn to choose certain behaviors over others. When a dog or cat acts incorrectly, it will learn that bad things happen, such as hearing your angry tone of voice, leash correction, a startling squirt of water, being ignored, or the absence of treats or other rewards.

Startle punishments are meant to stop an animal in the act before it is completed. Some of these include using a shake can (pennies in an empty soda can with the hole taped shut), tossing keys, squirting water or lemon juice from a small squirt bottle, a loud clap of hands, or a sudden, loud "No!" (Use this word only for startle command situations.) Or try the unexpected: Add unpleasant tastes, such as Bitter Apple or Tabasco sauce, on forbidden objects that your pet thinks are good to taste, chew, bite, or steal. Try placing sticky tape, aluminum foil, plastic carpet runner (nub side up), or electric mats on undesirable surfaces or objects that their feet will touch, such as counter tops or furniture. Small, shallow, water-filled plastic or foil containers, or an unstable cardboard platform lined with empty aluminum cans also work wonders on forbidden counter tops as will a quick spritz of water from behind or the sudden noise from a can of compressed air. Animals can be harmed or poisoned from spoiled food or discarded drugs, chemicals, and sharp objects that they have retrieved from a garbage can or wastebasket. In addition to using waste containers with step-on or spring activated lids, mousetraps planted in wastebaskets or garbage cans will startle most foraging pets without harming them.

Many people inadvertently reinforce a dog's or cat's fears or aggressive behavior by trying to reassure the animal about the situation that is triggering the undesirable behavioral response. By holding the animal, petting it, and telling it in a soothing voice that "it is okay," the animal associates those pleasant sensations (positive reinforcement) with its *behavior* instead of with the *situation*. For example, if a pet shows fear by trembling or by aggression, such as growling, showing teeth, clawing, or biting, the behavior must be corrected. When the animal understands that it has behaved improperly, you can work on a new, positive association with the person or object that elicited the response.

Yawning acts as a stress reliever for dogs by briefly lowering blood pressure. Watching a human or another creature yawn can actually help reduce a dog's anxiety. Cat yawns don't necessarily mean anything more than they just got up from a nap! (Photo by Dee Coleman)

Chewing

Because of their intense desire to chew, as well as put everything in their mouths, puppies need as much supervision as you would give a toddler. An unsupervised, active puppy can easily choke on both edible and inedible objects, including a treat such as a pig's ear or rawhide knot from a bone.

Puppy- and kitten-proof your home the same way you would for a crawling toddler. Do not leave tempting things like leather shoes or handbags where they can be reached; check for dangling electrical cords and remove poisonous houseplants. Instead, provide your puppy with appropriate chew toys and your kitten with a small pot of organic grass, catnip or valerian. In order for the catnip to work, however, you must gently squeeze it between your fingers, grinding it slightly to release the oils. While most cats love catnip, it's interesting to note that most very young kittens do not react to catnip at all.

To prevent or solve problems:

- Spray houseplants with unpleasant-tasting sprays, such as Bitter Apple

- Offer appropriate chew toys and greens

- Keep the animal confined to a crate or small area when not supervised

- Play with your pet daily to prevent boredom

- Social isolation should be avoided as much as possible to prevent chewing from loneliness or frustration

Puppies will chew plants, grass, leaves, sticks, and flowers mainly out of curiosity, while cats see the plants as resembling prey, with their waving leaves and fuzzy-looking flowers. Although some pets will chew plants simply out of boredom, nibbling on plants can also help them to regurgitate parasites or help the intestines pass them. Instead, try adding fiber to your pet's diet in the form of steamed green beans, carrots, peas, pumpkin, fresh celery, or apples.

Teething puppies especially need something to chew. Since puppies do not know which items they should not chew, it is up to you to teach them. If your puppy starts to chew something inappropriate, tell her "Leave it!" in a firm voice and *immediately* offer her an appropriate chew, such as rawhide or a rubber toy. Praise her when she chews the correct thing, using a consistent praise word or phrase, along with the word "chew" or the object's name. (Example: "Good dog, chew *bone*!")

After a puppy grows out of the teething stage, the reasons for chewing change. Dogs chew from boredom, lack of exercise or mental stimulation, anxiety, or stress. This kind of chewing becomes habit. Dogs also chew our things because they have our scent on them. Try scenting new, appropriate toys for them by holding the object in your hands or rubbing them between your palms first.

Plants to avoid:

- Easter Lilies

- Poinsettias

- Cycads

- Philodendrons

- Mistletoe leaves and berries

- Juniper berries

- Holly

- Daffodils, tulips, and other spring bulbs

- Poisonous weeds such as deadly nightshade

- Grass that is treated with lawn chemicals

- Common household trash holds dangers as well, including peach and apricot pits, which contain cyanide

Photo by permission
Barb Zurawski

Dominance and Aggression

Dogs need rules to respect their owners as pack leaders. Teach your pet to sit before you give him his food, a treat, or before you walk out the door or through a doorway. A dominant dog mounts or places a front leg over the more submissive animal. Discourage dogs from jumping up on people when the puppy is young and teach him the command "Off!" Have him sit while greeting visitors or being petted and praise the dog only when he sits. Ask visitors to crouch or sit to greet your dog so the dog can reach and interact with them better. Teaching the command "Off" will also prevent jumping up on counters or car doors. Respond quickly and consistently to unwanted behaviors such as leg mounting or growling to prevent it from becoming a habit or escalating into more dangerous dominant behavior, such as biting.

Dogs and cats jump on furniture for status, as well as comfort. Cats jump on furniture and other high places because they instinctively feel safer high off the ground, away from potential harm and with a better view to find prey. Offer your cat suitable places to jump onto or perch, such as a multi-tiered cat tree or window seat. In multiple cat households, the top cat shows her social status by seeking out the highest places. Our furniture holds our scent, which can be comforting to both dogs and cats, especially if they're lonely or stressed. If you do not want your dog or cat on your furniture, teach that from the beginning. Only hold your pet on your lap when you are sitting on the floor and do not allow her to climb up on the furniture one time, and shoo her off the next. Be consistent in your rules!

Photo courtesy Peggy Farrell-Kidd

Safety First

❧ Young children should not play with pets without supervision.

❧ Do not exceed the cat or dog's petting threshold. Watch for body language that indicates the animal is reaching or has reached her threshold: for cats this includes attempts to leave, tensing muscles, twitching tail, or hissing. Dogs display this by pawing, mounting, grabbing clothes or skin with teeth, growling, lifting lips, or showing teeth.

❧ Avoid petting cats on their stomach, hips or feet. Avoid approaching a dog from the rear or suddenly touching one while asleep.

❧ Both cats and dogs feel threatened by direct stares. Dominant or alpha dogs, especially, will interpret stares as aggression. Introduce strangers to your dog by having your dog sit or lie down.

❧ Avoid a frontal approach or bending down and looking straight into a dog's eyes. Make sure the person greets your dog next to its side, signaling non-dominant or non-threatening body language.

❧ Allow your cat to make the first move. Many cats are more comfortable approaching unfamiliar people after they have had time to get used to them.

❧ Spay or neuter your pets, especially in multiple pet households.

❧ Do not encourage games of aggression, such as tug-of-war, mounting or play-biting.

❧ Spray unpleasant tastes such as Bitter Apple on skin or clothing to discourage your pet from placing its teeth on human skin or clothing (which an animal considers as an extension of human skin).

❧ Redirect play-aggression to appropriate toys.

❧ Swaddling a cat in a small tee shirt or sweater can sometimes help curb aggression.

Black faux fur fabric (A)
Backing fabric or an additional piece of faux black fur (B)
1 yard each of 4 contrasting colored faux fur fabrics (C)

Matching thread, quilting pins
Scrap paper and pencil
Heavy-duty, sharp needle

Finished size:	Fabric Base (A) and Backing Piece (B)	Yardage Needed
S: 45" x 56"	Cut A & B 47" x 58"	1-1/3 yards 54"fabric or 2 yards 60" fabric of each A and B
M: 50" x 62"	Cut A & B 52" x 64"	1/8 yard 60" fabric of each A & B
L: 55" x 70"	Cut A & B 57" x 72"	2 yards 60" fabric of each A & B

1. Cut four 11" squares from each piece of contrasting fur (C). Cut 18 bones (from patterns, page 111) in 3 different sizes from each piece of the remaining yardage of the 4 contrasting fabrics(C). Cut a black faux fur piece (A) that measures 51" x 63" for the base fabric.

2. Spread the base fabric out flat. Arrange the bones and squares on the base fabric in a pleasing pattern, alternating the angles of the bones and/or squares. Draw a diagram on the scrap paper indicating the color, size, and placement of the squares. Pin the bones onto each individual square and remove squares from the base fabric.

3. Machine- or hand-sew the bones on each square using a satin, wide zigzag, or overcast edge stitch. Remove all the pins as you sew. Following the diagram, replace the squares onto the fabric base, pinning securely in place. Hand-sew the squares onto the fabric base. (Optional: Using the appropriate needle, machine-sew the squares onto the fabric base by first sewing a straight running stitch around each square. After all the squares are securely basted, topstitch each with a zigzag or satin stitch. Remove all the pins.)

4. Cut a backing piece (B) measuring the same dimensions as the fabric base. Place the backing piece and appliquéd fabric base RST. Pin along the edges. Straight stitch around the edges, allowing a 1/2" to 1" seam. Leave a 12" opening along one edge to turn. Turn RSO. Hand-sew the opening shut.

Spraying and Marking

Non-neutered or spayed dogs and cats mark or spray to cover up another dog's or cat's scent as a gesture of either sexual or territorial dominance.

To avoid problems with spraying and marking:

- Get pets neutered or spayed.

- Cover up previous scent with an enzymatic cleaner.

- Avoid using ammonia to clean, which smells like urine to your pet.

- Use a short lead and keep your dog walking, instead of allowing him to stop and mark.

- If you catch your dog or cat in the act, show disapproval with a loud clap, a loud and firm "No!", a shake can or other sudden startle technique. Then bring him immediately to the litterbox or outside to finish and praise him if he does.

- Spray your cat with a mist bottle or use a loud sound, as long as the cat cannot see that the punishment originates from you. (Do this only while the cat is in the act of spraying or marking.)

- Make an already marked area inaccessible or unsuitable by rearranging the furniture or placing the food bowl near where the marking has occurred.

House-Soiling

To prevent or solve problems with house-soiling:

- Shorten the stretches between dog bathroom breaks.

- Use an odor remover to eliminate the scent from previous accidents.

- Reinforce the positive only: Praise dogs when they eliminate outside or cats for using the litterbox. (Do not show anger for house soiling *after the fact!*)

- Help eliminate dog's submissive urination by reducing the excitement of your coming and going, as well as asking visitors to keep their greetings to the animal low-key.

- Take the pet to the veterinarian if you suspect physical reasons.

- Neuter or spay pets to reduce or eliminate marking.

- During periods of stress or change, keep your pet confined to one room at first and introduce new areas, a new baby, etc., slowly over a period of several days.

Aging Pets

With responsible ownership and good health, cats and dogs can be an important part of our lives for many years. A graying muzzle, bad breath, or less diligent grooming may be some of the first signs that a pet is aging. Occasional, but more frequent housebreaking mistakes are also common in an older pet. The onset of arthritis, vision and hearing loss, or cataracts parallels human aging, as well as the possibility of having more difficulty fighting infectious diseases, or developing chronic diseases such as diabetes, hyperthyroidism, or cancer.

How to care for an aging pet:

🐾 Increase the frequency, as well as the time, effort, and care spent in grooming sessions.

🐾 Check for lumps, sores, bad breath, weight loss or other signs of ill health by examining your pet regularly.

🐾 Monitor your pet's food and water intake. Take extra steps, if necessary, to make food more appealing and keep water fresher by changing it more often.

🐾 Adjust your pet's diet for specific medical problems. Use senior formula dog or cat foods.

Death of a Pet ... Dealing With Loss
Flesh not of my flesh,
Four legs instead of two.
And, yet, as if they were my own,
I loved every inch of you.
You trusted me, as I loved you,
My loyal, faithful friend.
And though you left my side too soon,
Your memory will never end.
                    Gail Green

Whether by accident, natural causes or by the difficult decision of euthanasia, the death of a pet can be felt as deeply as the loss of a human friend. Acknowledging your grief and allowing yourself adequate time to grieve will help you heal. Non-pet owning friends may not be sympathetic or understanding about the death of a beloved pet. Grief counselors specializing in pet loss, as well as pet loss support groups, can help you deal with your loss and get through this very difficult time.

Some pet owners get comfort from obtaining a new pet almost immediately after their loss while others need more time. Adopting again is a personal decision. The new pet will not take the place of the deceased, but welcoming in a new friend can often help fill that empty void and bring joy out of your sorrow.

How Pets Grieve

Our pets are as individual as humans, each with their own personalities and experiences. If you had a multiple pet household, your other animals may also be grieving as well, especially if the deceased was inseparable from another pet or pets. Although individuals will grieve in their own way, a personal glimpse into how real our pet's grief can be appears on the following page.

(Photo courtesy Katie Green)

(Photo permission
In Focus Imagery,
Jeff Green)

Madison died this morning. He had finally been seizure-free for five months and feeling so much better than he had in years. But, sometime in the early morning, he apparently had a seizure with complications and never woke up. We will never know if it was a stroke, heart attack, or he just stopped breathing, but the veterinarian assured us that there was nothing anyone could have done, even if we had been standing right there at the time.

Our two dogs, Tyler and Madison, were the best of friends. They had shared everything for years, from toys and bones to licking the stew pot clean together. Poor Tyler had to lie in his crate, just a few feet from Madison, watching him die … and then stay there until we came down this morning to discover our loss. Tyler has spent most of the day shaking and hiding. Madison's custom-made, bottomless crate was carefully moved from its normal spot in the kitchen into the family room.

Tonight, Tyler came out of hiding and walked over to the crate in the family room. I watched as he carefully sniffed the sidebars and then, unsure and confused, went over to the crate door to sniff. With one startled cry, he suddenly leaped back, as if he had been shocked by electricity. He then slowly walked to the kitchen where the crate had always been. After sniffing the spot on the floor for a few seconds where Madison had slept, he skulked away, ears back and tail carried low. Again he hid. About an hour later, he returned to "Madison's spot," sniffed the floor once, then sighed and lay down. Slowly, Tyler found the place on the wall where Madison used to lay against his crate bars, in the same position every night. I then watched as Tyler proceeded to lick that spot on the wall, over and over and over again, kissing his dear friend good-bye in a poignant gesture of farewell. Witnessing Tyler's silent grief was the saddest thing I have ever experienced.

It was days before we could get Tyler to eat. We finally resorted to hand-feeding him on our lap, away from the kitchen and its memories. As the days passed, we slowly moved closer and closer to his normal feeding place in the kitchen, until he was comfortable eating there again. Eventually, he began feeding out of his own food dish. It took weeks before Tyler was his old happy self again. A year later, we got another puppy. The two are now inseparable.

THE CAT AND DOG LOVER'S IDEA BOOK

Glue round and heart-shaped acrylic faceted stones onto the lid of a small painted wood box to create a memory box. Add decorative trim around the edges, if desired, or follow the additional creative options.

Creative *Options:*

• Write the name of your pet in the center of the lid using tacky glue and sprinkle glitter or tiny beads over it while still wet.

• Write your pet's name with an embossing pen, sprinkle embossing powder over it and heat to emboss.

• Use foiling adhesive and foil.

• Line the inside of the box with scraps of satin, gluing the edges to secure.

• Paint a glass, metal or ceramic box instead, using the appropriate painting supplies.

• Present as a gift box (with an additional gift inside) to a pet-loving friend.

• Create a larger box to use as a memorial box to hold keepsakes, your kitten or puppy's baby teeth or the ashes of a departed friend.

Photo courtesy Marilyn Manning

Chapter 4

LOOKING GOOD AT HOME ... AND AWAY!

Important Note: Make sure you use health care, insect control, and/or grooming products specifically labeled "feline" on cats and "canine" on dogs. (Photo courtesy Linda Ziegler)

Looking Good at Home

Grooming

Some pets need more grooming than others, especially if they have long or double coats. Introducing them to the clippers, nail file, and scissors with treats and praise will help make it a pleasant association.

Grooming is a wonderful way to bond with your pet. When they are very young, begin to get them used to being handled and groomed. Lightly brush or comb your pet, plus touch their teeth and pretend to trim nails daily. Introducing them to the clippers, nail file, and scissors with treats and praise will help make it a pleasant association.

Cats and dogs can have up to three types of fur in their coats. Some pets need more grooming than others, especially if they have long or double cots. Bathing and combing or brushing your cat or dog can reduce shedding, odor, incidence of hairballs in cats, and helps you to keep track of the condition of your pet's skin and general health. Groom longhaired dogs and cats daily to prevent mats from forming. Brush out short to medium coated cats and dogs once or twice a week. While wire or bristle brushes or slickers work well on dogs, choose a fine-toothed comb *only* for your cat, plus a natural bristle pin brush for grooming long hairs, such as the Maine Coon and Persian. Daily brushing of dogs going through seasonal shedding can significantly reduce the amount of fur deposited all over your home.

Cats spend thirty to fifty percent of their waking hours grooming themselves to distribute scent and oils, remove parasites, release tension and to help keep cool. Unless they are infested with fleas or have gotten into something very dirty, cats rarely need to be bathed. However, it is good to get your cat used to being bathed in the event that it is necessary at some point. Plus, bathing a cat weekly in clear water can help keep dander levels lower, and help keep allergies under control. When bathing a cat, make sure you use shampoo made especially for cats. Gently spray your cat with water while she stands in a tub or sink. Do not try to immerse her or make her stand in a tub of water. Dogs can be bathed easily in a shower, using a hand-held sprayer, or by standing in an empty tub and having clean water carefully poured over them to rinse. Take special care not to get soap or water in your pet's eyes or ears.

Hairballs can result when cats ingest fur during self-grooming. They are a common problem among the longhaired breeds and are the most common reason a cat will vomit. Signs of a hairball problem and possible impaction include retching, inability to defecate, diarrhea, loss of appetite or a swollen abdomen. Consult your veterinarian immediately if you suspect your cat is impacted. Increasing the fiber in your cat's diet, or adding small amounts of canned pumpkin, can help cats "pass" hairballs. Daily brushing, followed by wiping their coats with a moist rag, will lessen the amount of loose hair your cat will swallow.

Nails and Feet

Since dogs do not retract their nails, long nails can damage floors or make it difficult for the dog to walk. Keeping a cat's nails trimmed helps cut down on the desire to scratch and on the damage done by digging claws into things. Keep styptic powder nearby when trimming nails to stop bleeding quickly if you accidentally cut into the quick. And, make sure that nail trimmers are the right size for your pet.

Handling your pet's feet can be less stressful if you begin with the back feet. Press on the pad of one toe to expose a cat's nail; for dogs, just hold the toe still. Position the clipper just outside the quick, only cutting off the hook. Follow trimming by gently filing. Many dogs also need to have the hair between their toes trimmed. Check their pads regularly for signs of cracking, cuts or infections. Trimming underneath your dog's feet can help prevent balls of ice from forming between their toes when they are outside walking or playing in the snow.

Teeth

Brushing your dog's or cat's teeth regularly with special canine or feline toothpaste helps reduce plaque and tartar buildup (the primary source of gum disease), as well as stimulating the gums. Do not use human toothpaste on dogs or cats. Tooth brushing for cats and dogs should begin when young. First, let your kitten or puppy become used to having you putting your fingers in her mouth and rubbing her teeth. Once your pet is comfortable with

Brushing your dog or cat's teeth is a very important step in promoting a lifetime of healthy gums and preventing dental disease or tooth loss. (Photo courtesy Linda Ziegler)

that, introduce her to the taste of the toothpaste on a finger toothbrush or a soft child's toothbrush. For kittens and puppies, a soft cloth or gauze is a good way to introduce tooth brushing.

... and Away!

Travel and Car Rides

It is good practice to get your puppy or kitten used to car rides, other than trips to the veterinarian, when they are young. Frequent, short rides, ending in praise and treats, help them to anticipate car rides as enjoyable, rather than fearful, outings. Keep puppies in a travel crate and kittens in a carrier. This gives them a feeling of security, and prevents them from interfering with your driving safety. Pets who associate car rides with treats, praise, and fun times often grow up loving them!

Exercise caution during warm or extremely cold weather. *Never leave your pet in a parked vehicle when it is warm outside without open windows!* Temperatures in closed-up cars in the summer months can soar quickly and prove fatal.

Tips for traveling:

• An empty stomach can prevent car sickness.

• Carry a "pet kit" when traveling, in case of an emergency (see list, page 40).

• Keep pets strapped in, or confined to a travel crate or carrier, for longer trips. Make frequent stops and always keep your cat or dog on a leash in unfamiliar places.

• Make sure your dog or cat wears a collar with an ID tag that has been imprinted with your home phone number and emergency contact information, as well as any medications the pet needs.

• Stay overnight only in places where pets are welcome. Call ahead to avoid being stranded in an unfamiliar area without accommodations.

• For safety's sake, your dog should not put its head out of the window or ride in the back of an open truck.

Pet Kit List:

First aid kit
Water (preferably bottled)
Food (this is not the time to switch diets)
Disinfectant
Food/water bowls
Paper towels
Plastic bags
Cooler with ice
Health certificate, if traveling on a commercial airline
Veterinarian and vaccinations records (make sure vaccinations are up-to-date)
Crate or carrier

Bedding
Toys
Collar with ID
Leash (plus one extra leash)
Clean towels
Can opener (if using canned food; be sure to discard any leftover food)
Photo of pet in case it gets lost
Medication, especially if taken regularly (all prescription medications, including once a month heartworm prevention and medications to keep your pet calm)
For cats only: litterbox, litter, scoop

Getting Your Dog or Cat Used To Wearing a Collar or Walking on a Leash

Always use the proper collar on your pet. Dog collars are designed to prevent escapes, while cat collars are made to open easily to allow escapes. Make sure the collar fits snugly but still allows you to slide one finger underneath for a cat or small dog and two to three fingers under for a larger dog. Add ID tags with your phone number and address in case your cat or dog accidentally gets out.

Teach your dog or cat to walk properly with a leash. Felines should be walked with a leash and harness, rather than a leash and collar. Since leash pulling is a difficult habit to break, you'll want to prevent it from forming. Keep your dog's attention focused on you when walking. Bring along treats to keep him close to you, or play little games of catch with his favorite ball during your walk, A brisk game of fetch or Frisbee before a walk will often tire a very energetic dog enough to prevent him from wanting to pull.

Pins, Buttons, and Decorative Collars And Neckwear

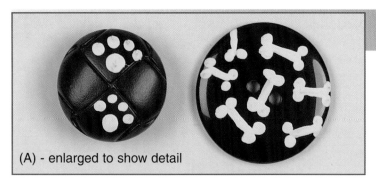

(A) - enlarged to show detail

BUTTON JEWELRY

Create these cat and dog pins by decorating ordinary 2- and 4-hole buttons with paint, small paper, leather or felt cutouts, metallic confetti or glued-on gems, beads or pompoms. Insert 26-gauge wire for cat whiskers and wiggle eyes or beads for a bit of whimsy! Glue on a jewelry pin-back and wear as a hatpin, tie tack or light-hearted brooch. (B)

Creative Options:

• Paint animal details on the buttons with fabric or dimensional paint.

• Paint bones or paw prints on buttons with paint for decorative accents on clothing. (A)

• Glue decorated and plain buttons onto wooden frames or other hard, decorative items.

(B)

MEN'S SILK TIES

The tie on the left was made by stamping a solid cat face from the template on page 111. Small wiggle eyes were glued onto each face using jewelry glue. The colorful tie on the right sports a rubber-stamped cat silhouette in rainbow fabric ink with stenciled clouds.

Photo courtesy Barb Zurawski

(Silk tie blanks Janlynn Corp./Arty's)

STRETCHY RUFFLED COLLAR

Note: These collars are to be used for adornment only.

1/8 yard of satin or other decorative fabric
Elastic (1/4", 1/2", or 3/8" width)

1. Cut two (3", 3-1/2", 4") wide pieces of fabric (2-1/2, 3, 4) times your pet's neck measurement. Fold the short edges under 1/2". Press or stitch in place.

2. Place RST, matching edges. Pin and stitch the long edges together. Turn RSO.

3. Cut a piece of elastic (1-1/2", 2", 2-1/2") larger than the measurement of your pet's neck. Insert the elastic into the fabric collar, gathering the collar around the elastic. Overlap the ends of the elastic 1" and pin into place. Stitch through both layers of elastic, and then slip the stitched ends into the ruffle so they aren't visible.

Creative Options:

- Use two contrasting colors for each side of the collar.

- Sew tiny bells or beads along the outer edge of the collar.

- Sew decorative trim into the long outer edge.

BEADED EVENING FLEECY COLLAR

6 mm white or cream pearl beads
4 mm and 6 mm assorted colored round beads
Scrap of blanket fleece and thread to match
Embroidery floss (six-strand) in the color of your choice
Needle to fit through beads
1" of hook-and-loop tape
Optional: Fabric or gem glue to glue on beads

1. Cut two (1", 1-1/4", 1-1/2") wide strips of fleece, per collar measurement instructions. Set one strip aside.

2. Sew on beads as follows: Insert the threaded needle in the center of one strip and come up to the RS. Thread six different color 4 mm beads onto the thread. Insert the needle back into the first bead on the strand to draw the beads into a circle. Tack in place on the fleece. Tack a pearl in the center of the circle.

3. Repeat Step 2, creating more pearl-centered circles every 1" to 1-1/2" until you are 2" from each of the short ends. Tack a single colored 6 mm bead between each cluster.

4. Match and place the second strip of fleece on the WS of the beaded strip. Cut 18" of floss and separate it into two 3-strand lengths for stitching. Matching the edges carefully, stitch through both layers along the edges with a running stitch, or other decorative stitch. Sew the hook-and-loop tape onto the short ends.

Creative Options
• Create a matching beaded choker necklace or headband for yourself.

• Experiment with different beaded patterns.

• Paint faux beads on, using dimensional fabric paint.

SHOWGIRL COLLAR

by Diane Schroeder

Using size 11/0 seed beads, make two identical double-beaded bands in the exact measurement of your pet's neck. Attach the band together with a triple row net-stitch or other decorative beading stitch. Weave ribbon into each end to lace the collar closed.

RIBBON EMBROIDERED COLLAR

by Diane Schroeder

Embroider flowers onto a 7/8" wide black velvet ribbon for a dramatic, elegant look! In sample shown, each flower has six Loop Stitch petals with a French knot center, three Lazy Daisy stitched leaves and a stem stitched stem.

POMPOM COLLAR

For an easy-to-make festive collar, thread tinsel pompoms onto an elastic cord. Use different colors and vary the sizes of the pompoms. Add a small jingle bell, if desired.

Creative Options

• Use several colors to make a multi-colored collar.

• Vary the sizes of the pompoms.

• String large beads in between the pompoms.

CANINE JUNGLE BANDANA

Make a "wild" fashion statement for your pet by gluing a fleecy felt shape onto a jungle print bandana (see general instructions page 7). Add beads for a nose and eyes, as well as a sparkling gold cord bow.

Creative Options

• Add fringe or other trim to short edges of bandana.

• Personalize by writing name of your pet using dimensional paint.

• Use the mouse pattern/template on page 111 to create a feline version.

Luxurious Faux Fur Collar

1/3 yard faux fur
3/4" circle or 1" square piece of sew-on, hook-and-loop tape
Quick grab fabric* or hot glue
Decorative button
Matching thread

* Gem-Tac or Fabri-Tac Permanent Adhesive (Beacon Chemical Co.)

1. Cut a rectangular strip of fabric to the correct measurement as follows: (4", 6", 8") wide times the length of your dog's neck + (3", 4", 5").

2. Fold each corner in 1" and sew or glue in place. Fold the short edges and the long edges in 1/2" and sew, or glue, as well.

3. Run a line of glue along one long edge, just inside the folded seam line. Fold the strip in half lengthwise and press to secure.

4. Sew the hook-and-loop tape onto each short end, just below the folded edge. Sew the decorative button on the collar, as shown.

Braided Collar

Beginning with lengths twice as long as your pet's neck size, braid 3 different colored trims, ribbons or laces for an unusual decorative collar. Stitch ends to secure and fasten with hook and loop tape or plastic clasp.

Decorating Purchased Web or Leather Collars and Leashes

Note: Use Gem-Tac Permenent Adhesive or other jewelry or leather glue to fasten items

A. Paint bones (connect 2 sets of twin dots with a straight line) in a random pattern using decorative paint.

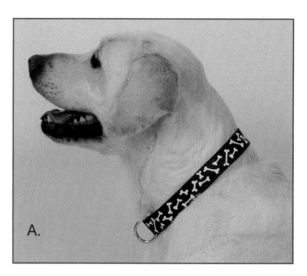

A.

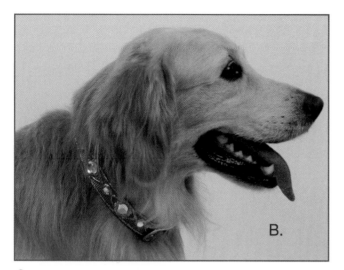

B.

B. Glue faux gems and jewels onto a collar. Let dry. Outline and embellish with gold or other metallic dimensional fabric paint.

C. Paint dots, squiggles or other abstract designs on the collar with dimensional paint.

C.

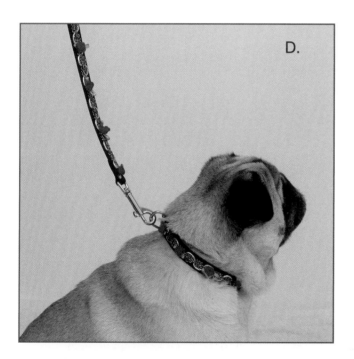

D.

D. Glue decorative ribbon trim onto a collar and leash. Glue small ribbon roses as desired over the ribbon.

E. Glue or sew narrow a width embroidered ribbon onto collar. Add a lace trimmed edge, if desired.

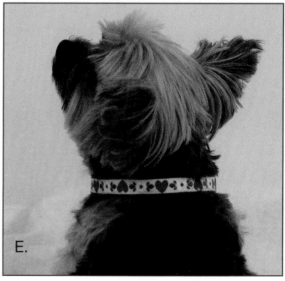

E.

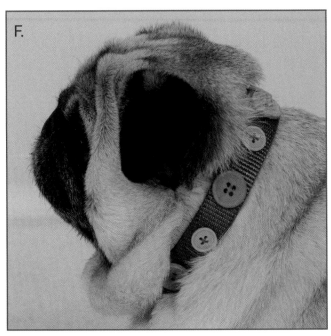

F.

G.

F. Sew colorful buttons on a web collar.

G. Add a detachable fleecy bone bow to a ready-made or ribbon-stamped collar as follows: Cut two (4-1/2", 5-1/4", 6" long) bones from the pattern on page 111 and one 1" x (5", 6", 7") strip of fleece. Put both bones together and hand- or machine-sew an overcast or other decorative stitch around the edges, 1/4" from the edge. Sew 1" squares of hook-and-loop tape to the ends of the fleece strip. Glue the strip to the back of the fleece bow, WST. Glue on decorative trim, additional felt appliqués, pompoms, ribbons, and buttons or sew on beads or decorative stitching.

H.

I.

H. Roll or sponge a pigment-ink rainbow over a flat, leather collar for a subtle but colorful look. Dry thoroughly before wearing. Decorate further, if desired, by stamping bones, paw prints or another image using textile ink and embossing.

I. Glue or sew ribbon over wide ruffled lace and attach to a ready-made or ribbon collar. Add a bell or other decorative accent.

Decorative Sweatshirts and Sweaters

NEON BONES DOG SWEATSHIRT

6 squares Shaggy Plush Felt in neon* or other colors of your choice
Scrap of paper
Black sweatshirt in a size to fit the length of your dog
Washable fabric glue **
Tee-shirt board
Tailor's chalk

* Shaggy Plush Felt: Groovy Green, Marmalade Sky, Purple Passion, Moody Blue (Kunin Felt, A Foss Manufacturing Company, Inc.)
**Fabri-Tac Permanent Adhesive (Beacon Chemical Company)

1. Try the sweatshirt on the dog. Mark the sleeve above the ankle. Remove the sweatshirt and cut the sleeves as marked. Turn the cut edge under 3/8" and glue in place. Let dry.

2. Using the template on page 111, cut out bones in assorted colors. Place the sweatshirt on the tee-shirt board. Arrange the bones in three or four rows across the front of the sweatshirt, varying the colors and angles. Glue each bone in place. Let dry on the board.

3. Flip the board over and glue more bones in three or four rows onto the back of the sweat shirt. Remove from the board when dry.

4. Inside each sleeve, insert a piece of scrap paper cut in the shape of the sleeve. Keeping the sleeve flat, glue bones on both sides and top of each sleeve. Remove paper when dry.

Creative Options:

• Machine- or hand-sew the edges and appliqué bones on instead of gluing. Or use iron-on adhesive or fusible web.

• For male dogs: Remove the band from the bottom of the sweatshirt, turn the edge over and stitch to form a 1" casing. Slip a drawstring or shoelace into the casing or measure elastic to the girth of your dog and stitch after inserting. Check that it isn't too tight by making sure that you can insert two or three fingers underneath the bottom edge.

• Decorate the sweat shirt using appliqués created from different templates found on page 109-111.

• Paint or stamp bones (or other designs) on a lighter colored sweatshirt.

CANINE HOOD
TOPPER

1/2 yard of fleece fabric that does not have a
right or wrong side
1-1/2" piece of hook-and-loop tape
Tape measure
Tailor's chalk

1. Measure your dog's head, as shown in General Instructions, page 6. Add 1" to the measurement and cut out a rectangle (11", 13", 15") long by your measurement plus 2".

2. Fold the rectangle in half lengthwise. Stitch around the edges, 1/2" from the edge, leaving 2" open to turn. Turn and top stitch around the edges, 1/4" from edge, stitching the opening shut as you sew.

3. Wrap the rectangle around your dog's head. Using tailor's chalk carefully mark where the base of each ear is located. Remove the fabric. Cutting through both layers, cut two 3/4" deep slits, matching the measurement for the width of your dog's ears. Satin stitch the edges around the ear slits.

Photo permission In Focus Imagery,
Jeff Green

4. Separate the hook-and-loop tape. Place 1 piece in each of the corners on the folded edge. Stitch in place.

Creative Options:

• Decorate the hood to match any of the other decorated sweaters.

• Decorate the hood with beads, appliqués or paints.

• Monogram your pet's name or initials on the hood.

• Make a matching hood for yourself (without the ear slits, of course).

• Make the hood reversible. Instead of cutting one large piece and folding it, cut two narrower pieces out of contrasting fabric and stitch all the edges together. Or stitch the hood out of a different fabric, such as velvet or faux fur.

RIBBON ROSES, SNOWFLAKES AND TASSEL FRINGE

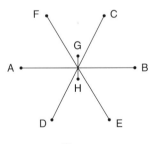

Diagram

Embroidered Snowflakes:
Embroider sparkly snowflakes onto a sweater using white glittery yarn and the simple embroidery technique, shown in the Diagram.
For each snowflake: Insert yarn into tapestry needle and knot end of yarn. Come up through A and down at B, up at C and down at D, up at E and down at F, up at G and down through H. Tack in place on the WS of the sweater.

(Yarn from Lion Brand Yarn)

Tassel Fringe:
Buy or create custom color tassels to match favorite school or sports team colors, using an assortment of types and/or weights of yarns and sewing them around the sweater's collar.

Ribbon Roses:

Note: One 15" length of wire-edged ribbon or ribbon with a gathering stitch sewed along one long edge makes one rose. Make as many ribbon roses as desired, depending on the size of your pet and/or sweater.

1. Carefully begin to pull the wire (or thread) from both ends along the same edge, gathering the ribbon toward the center as you go. (Tip: Pull out 1/2" wire only to start, then twist the ends together to keep the wire from slipping out of the edge.)

2. When the ribbon is completely gathered, squeeze the gathered, curled edge together and wrap the wire or thread around it (1/2" from the edge) to secure.

3. Twist the curled ribbon to form the rose shape. Trim excess wire or thread. Sew each rose securely onto the sweater.

Cold Weather Tips:

🐾 Consider the wind chill factor before leaving your dog outside.

🐾 Exercise caution when playing or walking near frozen lakes or rivers.

🐾 Single- or short-coated dogs, as well as puppies or seniors, may need extra protection from the cold, such as a sweater or coat.

🐾 Dogs that are active in cold weather burn more calories and might need an increase in their diet.

🐾 Do not leave your dog very long in a car during cold weather or unattended with the car engine running.

🐾 Check for ice that can build up between the toes, as well as cuts from walking on icy ground. If you walk him in areas where road or sidewalk salt has been used, wash your dog's paws as soon as you return so he will not ingest any residue when cleaning them himself.

Make sure your pet has adequate shelter from the elements when outside. Dogs should not stay outside without shelter longer than it takes to "do their business" on hot, cold, rainy or snowy days. Adjust outdoor activity according to the weather. Heavy coated or breeds with black or dark coats cannot take the heat and humidity. Conversely, light-coated and short-muzzled breeds get chilled and can develop hypothermia easily in temperatures below 20 degrees. Watch out for your cat in the summer or winter months, as well to ensure she hasn't accidentally gotten locked into the attic or garage or other hot or cold area. (Photo courtesy Pat Schulz)

REVERSIBLE COZY CANINE COAT

1 yard each of Berber Fleece in two contrasting fabrics
1 yard of hook-and-loop tape
Matching thread
Large sheet of paper (or brown paper bag that has been opened up per General Instructions, page 6)

1. Measure your pet as per General Instructions, page 6. Length: From the back of the neck to the beginning of the tail. Girth: The largest measurement around the chest, just behind the front legs. Chest: Across the chest, from shoulder to shoulder.

2. To make your pattern, enlarge the basic pattern pieces found on page 109 to a proportionate size that most closely matches the length measurement. Transfer or trace these pattern pieces onto a large sheet of paper. Check the other measurements and adjust, if necessary, across the front band, allowing for 1/2" seams and a (2-1/2", 3", 4") overlap. Redraw the angles and curves, if necessary, to fit. Check the stomach band length and adjust as well. Cut out the adjusted pattern pieces. Pin the pieces together and *check them on your dog before cutting out the fabric.*

3. Matching the main pattern piece against the fold, cut out a full body piece from each of the two fabrics. Cut out two stomach band pieces from each fabric as well. Place the contrasting stomach band pieces RST and stitch around the long edges of each pair, leaving the short ends open to turn. Turn RSO.

4. Place the two body pieces RST and pin, inserting the two stomach bands where indicated on the pattern. Carefully, try the coat on your pet again, adjusting band placement, if necessary. Stitch around the edges, double reinforcing the bands and leaving 3" open to turn. Turn RSO.

5. Sew triple and double rows of (2", 4", 6") hook-and-loop tape where indicated on the stomach and chest bands.

Creative Options:

• Use felt instead of fleece. Using the patterns on pages 109 to 111, appliqué a dog silhouette, paw prints, or bones, out of contrasting felt colors.

• Make a leopard print or mink faux fur jacket. Trim the collar with faux diamonds or pearls.

• Make a matching Canine Hood Hat (page 48).

Outdoor cats and dogs are more likely to pick up parasites, such as fleas or hookworm, than indoor ones and should be checked regularly, along with their bedding, for evidence of fleas, especially if they have skin irritations or are doing a lot of scratching or biting. Using a strong light and a flea comb, examine your pet's lower back, abdominal area or rump. Tiny black or brown specks (flea dirt) or shapes that jump around near the skin or on the bedding are usually telltale signs of the presence of fleas. Consult with your vet on methods to use to control or prevent fleas. Help prevent flea infestation by regularly vacuuming and washing pet areas and bedding, as well as yours, too, if you allow your pet in your bed or on the furniture. (Photo courtesy Barb and Burt Horowitz)

Hot Weather Tips:

🐾 Do not leave your dog unattended in direct sunlight or in a closed vehicle! If you must leave your dog in a car for even a short period of time, make sure that the windows are slightly open, that you are parked in the shade, and that he has water accessible to him.

🐾 Offer plenty of shade and water to prevent heat stroke.

🐾 Signs of heat stroke include panting, drooling, rapid pulse, and fever. If you think your dog has had heat stroke, immediately immerse the dog in cool water and seek emergency veterinary help.

🐾 Slow down activity in hot, humid weather, especially when it is sunny. Reduce exercise during the day and take walks instead in the early morning or evening.

🐾 Watch for insect bites or stings. Allergic reactions or multiple stings can require immediate veterinary care.

🐾 Be on the alert for access to poisonous garden plants including lily of the valley, larkspur, morning glory, and periwinkles.

🐾 Check daily for fleas and ticks.

🐾 Exercise caution to prevent ingestion or contact with garden products, and lawn fertilizers, treatments, or pesticides.

🐾 Shorthaired or lightly pigmented dogs can become sunburned. Use sun block before going outside, as well as limiting the amount of time outdoors during the middle of the day.

🐾 Supervise your pet around bodies of water, including rivers, lakes, and pools. Dogs with large, heavy heads, such as the Bulldog, can drown in as little as two feet of water.

CHILD'S REVERSIBLE VISOR AND MATCHING PET BANDANA

Attach 2 sheets of craft foam together using double-sided adhesive and cut out a visor from the template on page 110. Cut out a puppy and/or a kitty face out of shaggy or fuzzy felt or faux fur from the templates on page 111, or use a ready-made visor. Glue onto the visor as shown and add facial details (leather shoelace whiskers and pompom eyes and nose). Punch a hole at either end and insert a curly shoelace into the holes to hold the visor on your child's head. Make a matching bandana for your pet, following the general instructions.

CHILDREN'S SHOES

Canvas shoes in the size of your choice
Fabric paint (both dimensional and brush on)*
Paintbrushes
Stylus, eraser, and transfer paper**

* Fashion Dimensional and/or Brush-on Fabric Paint (Plaid Enterprises)
** Saral Paper Corp.

1. Using the transfer paper and stylus, trace over the outline of the dog or cat template (on page 111) and transfer onto each shoe.

2. Brush paint onto the solid areas of the head and ears. Let dry. Add eyes, nose and mouth. Let dry.

3. Outline images with corresponding color of dimensional paint, adding the dog's tongue, textural fur details, nose highlight, and cat's whiskers. Paint dots with dimensional paint to create random paw prints.

Creative Options:

• Paint one shoe with a dog, the other a cat.

• Glue pompoms on the shoes to match the visor.

• Paint a random pattern of bones or fish bones instead of paw prints.

Chapter 5

LET'S PLAY!

Note: All the toys in this chapter should be used with supervision!

Interactive Play

Both kittens and puppies engage in social play, as well as instinctive hunting play. Most cat and kitten play draws on instinctive predatory behavior, in which toys are viewed as "prey." Although the same predatory instinct exists in dogs, it is usually channeled into work, whether herding, hunting, or protectiveness and is augmented by their need for social hierarchy. Dogs engage in play through play biting, growling, and dominance play, including both male and female mounting.

Interactive play with a cat or dog can reduce over-excitement when you or other people are around. Although most dogs need thirty to forty minutes of exercise a day, some active breeds require even more. Dogs don't play very well alone and prefer human company rather than

Kittens and puppies get tired very easily and only play for short periods of time when they are very young. Never force your kitten or puppy to play when she wants to rest or sleep. (Photo courtesy Pat Schulz and Maureen Tobias)

being left out alone in a yard. Avoid playing tug-of-war games, especially if your dog does not clearly view the person playing as "pack leader." These types of activities can encourage dominance and sometimes aggression in more dominant or "alpha" dogs.

The mutual relationships pet owners enjoy with their pets need to be built by spending the time necessary. Start early by turning everyday activities into pleasurable experiences. (Photo courtesy Joe and Lynn Heidlinger)

Ideas for interactive play and games with your dog:

🐾 Play Frisbee or ball.

🐾 Go for long walks.

🐾 Participate in dog sports (see page 83).

🐾 Daily or weekly training sessions.

🐾 Go to a dog park.

🐾 Create a neighborhood dog playgroup with other friends' well-socialized dogs; meet regularly for both dogs and their humans to interact or go for walks together.

🐾 Give your dog a fun job to do, such as carrying in the newspaper or visiting nursing homes as a certified Therapy Dog.

🐾 Play decision-making or hide-and-seek type games to provide mental stimulation.

🐾 In bad weather, play indoors with squeaky toys, a soft Frisbee, or a ball.

🐾 Teach "find it" games using a treat and three inverted plastic cups: have your dog sit and stay. Place a treat under one cup and move all the cups around, mixing up the original order. Then tell your dog to "find it." Praise him when he finds the treat.

Taking time to play with your cat or dog each day will help reinforce your bond, as well as reduce stress and provide mental and physical exercise.

(Photo courtesy Dee Coleman)

Cats need much of the same mental stimulation and interactive playtime with their owners. Use interactive "prey" toys, such as those shown on pages 57-59 to provide them with a fun activity to do while you are watching television or chatting on the phone. To hold your cat's interest, make the toys always "new" by using just a few toys during each play session and pulling out a different set of toys to play with every few days.

Interactive toys should be put away when playtime has ended. Yarn, string, ribbons or tinsel should never be offered as a toy for a pet to play with. Ingesting these materials can cause serious and possibly fatal results. Supervise your chewing puppy or curious kitten to prevent it from ingesting garbage, poisons, chemicals, small objects or large chunks of rawhide that might be hard to pass, or outside dangers, such as ingesting poisonous plants or parasite-containing rabbit or goose droppings.

Interactive and Recyclable Toys for Pennies or Less

Dogs:

• Empty, clean plastic two-liter soda pop bottles, half-gallon or gallon milk jugs, sixty-four ounce or larger plastic apple juice bottles are great supervised puppy toys. (Remove labels and caps before offering toy to pet.) Add a treat or two inside the container for more fun. Throw away when puppy begins to chew them or they show signs of damage.

• Drill a hole through a tennis ball. Insert 1" thick, heavy-duty rope and knot at teach end. (Wet the rope to insert.)

Cats:

• Empty spool of thread, wadded up ball of aluminum foil, or empty paper grocery bag or paper box. (Check for staples!)

• Plastic safety ring from gallon milk jugs or plastic holder from soda can 6-packs.

• Cut holes in a box and insert something inside to poke at, such as a pompoms, balls, etc.

• Cut a slit in the cover of an empty, clean margarine tub. Place a ping-pong ball or large bell inside the container and secure the lid shut with glue or double-sided tape.

*Create a **Mylar Crinkle Ball** by placing four 3-1/4" x 4-1/2" Mylar rectangles on top of each other. Beginning with the short end, fold up accordion-style, creating 1/4" folds. Twist a chenille stem in the center to secure. Trim and pull out each layer to form a ball shape. Or cover an empty cardboard toilet paper roll with metallic Mylar to make a **Rolly Crinkle Toy.** Squeeze the tube slightly before rolling to release the sound. This unusual crinkle sound will entice most cats to play.*

More Cat Toy Ideas...

• Use a flashlight to create dancing, moving light "prey" for your cat to chase around the walls and floors. Once in awhile, cover or turn off the light and then make it reappear somewhere else.

• Place a ball or balls in the bathtub, sink, or in a large plastic container that will not tip over.

• Cut holes in an empty, clean soda bottle and insert something inside to poke at that rattles and makes noise, such as small balls of aluminum foil.

• String fish-line or a leather shoelace through a long straw. Tie feathers or other dangly objects at the end.

• Cut several curly ponytail holders in half. Bundle them together, using floral tape, and attach to a stick or long straw.

• Pompoms, especially sparkly ones, make great "prey." Glue chenille stems and pompoms together to create "creatures."

• Make wobbly toys by partially filling snap-apart plastic Easter eggs with uncooked rice; glue shut. Drill or poke a hole into the top of the egg. Glue feathers or short pieces of curly shoelaces into the hole.

• Create a curly chenille stem toy and attach it to an 18"-long dowel rod. Or glue a suction cup at one end and secure it to a table or floor.

• Glue a bundle of sanitized feathers to a 36" long dowel rod for a wonderful tease-and-pounce toy.

• Place a jingle bell inside an empty 35 mm film canister. Seal lid with glue or tape.

• Blowing bubbles will fascinate kittens, as well as puppies and many adult pets.

• Weighted plastic penguin bird toys also makes a good supervised kitten toy.

• Stitch a small fabric pouch or pillow and stuff with catnip.

• Roll a ball or an empty toilet paper tube across the floor.

Interactive Prey Toys for Cats

Glue a plastic practice golf ball onto each end of a curly shoelace. Or, substitute two colorful ping-pong balls for the practice golf balls. Drill a hole in each ball. Insert the shoelace ends into the holes and glue to secure.

JINGLE CUBE

Sew squares of colorful plastic canvas together into a cube, using colorful craft cord. Add a small jingle bell inside before stitching the final edge shut.

Shown: *Needleloft Craft Cord (Uniek) Solid Purple 55030 and Solid Magenta 55032

Glue six 2-1/2" leather strips, two 3-1/2" scrap faux fur or fleece circles and eight 5 mm pompoms together to form a spider shape. Attach to an 18"-long wooden dowel rod with fishing line. Stuff catnip inside the spider, if desired, before gluing it shut. Or, make a different shaped dangling toy, such as a mouse or fish shape; glue sanitized feathers on instead of leather strips.

SHINY TASSEL TWIRLER

Attach a taped metallic shred bundle to an 18" long dowel rod, using three feet of 24-gauge wire or a curly chenille stem. Just twirl this rod and watch your cat chase the spinning tassel.

Creative Options

• Insert leather or cord through the holes drilled through ping-pong balls; tie onto a dowel rod.

• Attach leather or faux fur strips onto a cord that is tied to a dowel rod.

• Glue a suction cup to a bundle of feathers; press onto a surface and let your cat "attack."

• Instead of fishing line, leather or cord, use 24-gauge wire attached to a 4" dowel rod "handle." Place the "handle" into a drawer and close to secure.

KNITTED OR CROCHETED EGG OR BALL

by Barb Zurawski

1. CO 10 stitches.

2. P 2 even rows.

3. K1 INC. Repeat 3 more times.

4. K1 INC, K2 INC. Repeat 6 more times. (18 ST)

5. K1 row, P1 row. Repeat once.

6. K1, K2 TOG; K2, K2 TOG. Repeat 3 more times. (14 ST)

7. K1, K2 TOG; K1, K2 TOG. Repeat 3 more times. (10 ST)

(Photo permission Barb Zurawski)

8. To finish: Insert a 12" length of yarn into a needle. Thread the yarn through each loop on the knitting needle, removing each loop as you go. Pull tight and tie together. Stuff with the ball with fiberfill and fresh dried catnip. Sew the sides together.

CAT-A-PILLAR TOY

by Dee Coleman
Scraps of sport or worsted yarn that are FDA approved, safe for infants or dyed with non-toxic dyes*
"G" or "H" crochet hook

* Jamie 3-ply baby sport and 4-ply worsted in assorted colors (Lion Brand Yarn)

1. Make a chain of 45 stitches.

2. Double crochet in the 2nd chain back.

3. Do 2 more double crochets in the same stitch.

4. Do 3 double crochet in each stitch to obtain the length desired, usually 2"- 3".

5. Finish off with a double crochet, then 2 single crochets.

6. Single crochet a tail 2" to 4" long. Tie a bell onto the end and tie a tight knot. Trim and fray the end.

Creative _Options:_
• Add another bell in the middle of the toy.

• Spray a catnip-scent onto the toy.

Soft Toys for Dogs

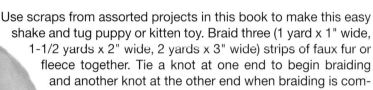

Use scraps from assorted projects in this book to make this easy shake and tug puppy or kitten toy. Braid three (1 yard x 1" wide, 1-1/2 yards x 2" wide, 2 yards x 3" wide) strips of faux fur or fleece together. Tie a knot at one end to begin braiding and another knot at the other end when braiding is complete.

CATCH-A-MOUSE

Scrap of gray and pink felt* or low pile faux fur or fleece
Needle and thread (gray, pink and black)
4-1/2" length black craft cord **
Polyester fiberfill
Optional: 1/4 cup of dried catnip

* Gray and pink Rainbow Shaggy Felt (Kunin)
** Needleloft Craft Cord (Uniek)

1. Trace and cut out the mouse pattern pieces (page 111). Trace the pattern shapes onto the gray felt or fur and cut out 2 gray mouse bodies, 2 gray mouse ears and 2 pink mouse ears.

2. Place the mouse ears WST, 1 pink and 1 gray piece. Top stitch around, 1/8" from edge. Satin stitch black eyes and a pink nose on each of the mouse body pieces, following pattern placement.

3. Sew each mouse ear onto a body piece, pink side up, as indicated on pattern. Place the mouse bodies together, WST. Insert 1/2" of the cord in between the two pieces, where indicated on the pattern. Stitch close to the edges and over the cord, leaving a 2" opening along the bottom seam.

4. Stuff with fiberfill and/or catnip, crushing the catnip between your fingers prior to inserting. Hand-sew shut. Tie a knot at the end of the tail.

Creative Options:

• Make the mouse in a soft velvet fabric instead.

• Omit the catnip and enlarge the pattern, if necessary, for a dog toy.

Iced Donut, Chocolate Chip Cookie, and Gingerbread Man Dog Toys

(Photo permission In Focus Imagery, Jeff Green)

For all three toys:
3/4 yard tan faux fur, fleece or felt *
1/4 yard brown fleece or felt *
1/4 yard off-white faux fur, fleece or felt *
Scraps of red and dark brown felt *
Polyester fiberfill
Black, off-white, red, tan, brown, orange, and green thread
Small crochet hook
White regular rickrack **
Animal safety squeaker ***
Scissors
Disappearing marking pen
#16 (Denim) sewing machine needle or sharp, heavy-duty needle for hand sewing (quilting or tapestry)

* Rainbow Plush Felt (Kunin Felt, A Foss Manufacturing Company): Cashmere Tan, Light Heather Brown, Dark Heather Brown, Antique White, and Red
** Wrights Trims
*** Zims, Inc.

Iced Donut
1. Cut out two (6", 8", 10") circles from the tan and one circle from the off-white fabric. Fold in quarters, RST, and find the center point. Marking it on the WS, trace a (1-1/4", 2", 2-3/4") circle in the center of each of the circles. Cut each center circle out by cutting into the circle from the outer edge. (Diagram).

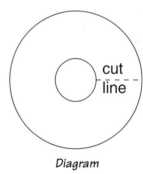

Diagram

2. Using the icing pattern as a guide and enlarged to the correct size, cut the free-form icing shape out of the off-white circle. Using a medium width stitch, satin stitch 3/4"–1" long sprinkles on the RS of the icing shape, in brown, orange, and green.

3. Place the completed icing on top of one of the tan circles and pin in place. Satin stitch around the icing edges with the off-white thread. Place the two tan circles RST. Straight stitch around the outer and inner curved edges, 1/4" from the edge. Stitch again to reinforce. Turn right side out.

4. Stuff the donut with fiberfill. Add an animal safety squeaker, if desired. Matching the seams, hand-stitch the opening shut.

Chocolate Chip Cookie

1. Cut out two (6", 8", 10") circles from the tan fabric. Cut out (six 1/2" to 3/4", seven 3/4" to 1", eight 1-1/2") brown circles.

2. Place the brown circles in a pleasing random pattern on the RS of one of the tan circles. Using a medium width stitch, satin stitch three-quarters of the way around one of brown circles. With your needle in a down position through the fabric, lift your pressure bar to release the foot. Insert a pinch of fiberfill into the brown circle, using the small end of the crochet hook to push it in. Replace your sewing machine foot. Finish stitching around the brown circle. Repeat satin stitching and stuffing for each of the brown circles.

3. Place the 2 tan circles RST. Straight stitch around the edges, 1/4" from the edge. Stitch again to reinforce. Turn right side out.

4. Stuff the cookie with fiberfill. Add an animal safety squeaker, if desired. Fold open edges in 1/4". Matching the seams, hand-stitch the opening shut.

(Photo permission In Focus Imagery, Jeff Green)

Gingerbread Man

1. Enlarge gingerbread boy and bow patterns, page 111. Cut out 2 gingerbread boy pattern pieces from the tan felt and two bows from the red felt.

2. Measure and place strips of the white rickrack across the head, arms and legs, as shown, on the RS of one of the gingerbread boy pieces. Straight stitch in place.

3. Mark the eyes and mouth on the right side of the piece with the disappearing marker. Satin stitch eyes and a mouth in black.

4. Topstitch the bow around the edges WST, using a narrow zigzag stitch. Sew the bow in place on the gingerbread boy by straight stitching two parallel lines in the center.

5. Place the second gingerbread boy piece onto the first, RST and matching edges. Straight stitch along the seam line around the entire outside of the toy, leaving the top edges open 2-1/2".

6. Carefully snip curves and turn RSO. Stuff lightly with fiberfill. Insert the squeaker just beneath the red bow. Add more stuffing and hand-stitch shut.

Chapter 6

LET'S EAT!

Feeding Our Pets

Cats and dogs are carnivorous and need a nutritionally balanced diet, containing protein and other nutrients found in meat. Puppies and kittens need extra nutrition in their first six to eight months of life to grow properly. Whether you prefer to feed your pet a commercially made food or a holistic, home-made diet, make sure to consult your veterinarian regularly regarding special nutritional needs during certain growth stages as well as when to switch to maintenance or lighter formulas.

Cats need almost twice the daily protein as a dog, with frequent small high protein meals throughout a day, while dogs are programmed to fast for many hours between infrequent large meals. Dry prepared food or kibble can be left out all day, if you prefer free-range feeding. Canned food, however, should only be left out for a short period of time and leftovers removed from the can and refrigerated promptly. Always have clean, fresh water accessible to your cat or dog during the waking hours.

(Photo permission Barb Zurawski)

Dogs' and cats' digestive systems are more sensitive to food changes than are humans' digestive systems. Gradually increase the daily proportions of a new food while simultaneously decreasing the old, to avoid the gastrointestinal upsets that can occur with sudden and multiple diet changes.

Like most Americans, many of our pets are overweight. If you cannot easily feel your pet's ribs and/or if a dog does not appear to have a defined waist, your dog or cat may be too fat.

Tips for Overweight Pets:

• Use treats sparingly, for special occasions or as training rewards.

• Vegetables, such as small carrot or celery pieces, or low-sodium canned or cooked frozen vegetables without onion seasoning are good, low-fat, healthy alternatives to "table scraps" and high calorie packaged treats.

• Decrease food amounts or switch to a lower calorie food.

• Increase exercise to burn calories; just be careful and go easy at first!

Free-range feeding (leaving food out and available all day) can often lead to over-eating, obesity or fussy eaters. Picky eating can often be avoided by not feeding your pet table scraps; unless that is the diet you will be consistently providing him. If you must, only offer your pet table scraps from *his* bowl, rather than from the table. Create specific meal times and remove uneaten food after fifteen minutes. Offer the remainder again, at the next regular mealtime, along with the additional meal.

There is no such thing as a free lunch, a free treat, pat on the head or playtime! In the wild the alpha (leader) canines eat first, followed by those next in the social ranks. Dogs and cats should *work* to get the things they want. Teach your puppy from the beginning that you are in charge by having him earn his food and wait until you give him permission to have it. Tell him to sit while you prepare his meal. Place the bowl on the ground in front of him and have him sit and stay until you tell him it is okay to eat the food in his bowl. All food or treats (including any table scraps) should be offered *only* from his bowl or directly from you so that your pet will learn his place in the "pack hierarchy."

If, however, you can see the ribs through the fur, or the animal's ribs and spine feel "bony," your pet may be too thin. Increase the daily amount of food or slowly change to a more calorie-laden formula. If your pet is refusing his food, mix in a flavor enhancer or enzyme supplement with his regular food or warm up his food to release the scent. Some pets prefer to eat with the rest of the family, for social reasons, as well as the stimulation of the scents and sounds of mealtime.

Non-neutered males and non-spayed females that are pregnant or are in heat often will not eat well. Lack of appetite is also a natural response to the death of another pet. Aging felines and those that are ill, underweight, or under stress often respond well to human baby food, which is portable, regulated and easy to digest. Pets that are stressed may also need to be temporarily hand fed.

Avoid exercising your dog one hour before or after it has eaten a meal to prevent it from developing stomach bloat, a serious and potentially fatal condition that affects primarily dog breeds with large chests. (Photo permission In Focus Imagery, Jeff Green)

THE CAT AND DOG LOVER'S IDEA BOOK

Chicken or turkey bones are brittle and should never be offered to cats or dogs, as they can splinter in your pets' throats and cause internal damage. Dogs also often eat things that they shouldn't and wind up throwing them up later. Take the trash out daily, keep garbage cans and wastebaskets covered, and provide adequate outdoor supervision to prevent your dog from eating harmful things. Feed two smaller meals a day, rather than one large meal to prevent voracious or rapid eating due to excessive hunger. If you change to a lower (or higher) calorie food, change food slowly over a series of days to avoid the results of a sudden change of diet. Dogs with digestive upsets often benefit from being placed temporarily on a simple cooked ground meat and rice diet.

Sometimes food stealing is due to hunger, especially in a growing or active pup or kitten whose nutritional needs aren't being met or whose food is not being digested properly, especially if the food contains too much indigestible ingredients or not enough protein. Parasites or hormone imbalances can also create ravenous appetites. Consult your veterinarian if your pet's appetite seems out of control, or if feedings are consistently followed by vomiting, loose stools, or signs of discomfort.

(Photo courtesy Linda Ziegler)

Tips for getting a dog (or cat) to take medicine:

- Keep pills in a treat jar to absorb the smell of his favorite treats.

- Wrap the pill in a small ball of cream cheese or canned food and offer it to him as a treat reward.

- Place pill in his mouth, on the back of his tongue; hold his muzzle tight and quickly blow in his nostrils or gently stroke his throat; release when you feel him swallow.

- Squirt liquid medicine into pet's mouth with a syringe.

Signs of illness:

- Lack of energy or unusual sleepiness.

- Changes in appetite, water consumption or grooming habits.

- Bathroom accidents, decreased or increased frequency of urination or change in consistency of stools.

- Behavioral changes, including aggression or lack of interest in favorite activities or playing.

- Gradual or sudden weight loss.

- Lack of coordination or awareness of surroundings.

- Dizziness, frequent falling or convulsions.

- Frequent vomiting, or non-productive vomiting.

Treats

General Note: Offer treats sparingly to avoid digestive upset or weight gain. The treats in this book do not contain any preservatives; therefore, refrigeration or freezing are highly recommended.

EASY SWEET BREATH BAGELS

Sweeten your best friend's breath with these easy-to-make treats! Makes 15-18.

Ingredients:
- 2 c. all-purpose flour
- 1/4 c. wheat germ
- 1/2 tsp. baking powder
- 1/2 c. fresh minced parsley or dried parsley flakes
- 1/4 c. fresh chopped peppermint leaves or 2 tbsp. peppermint extract
- 4 tbsp. canola oil
- 3/4 c. water

Directions

1. Mix the dry ingredients in a medium bowl and set aside.

2. Mix the oil, water and peppermint extract or chopped leaves in a small bowl and add to the dry ingredients. Mix together well to form dough.

3. Place the dough on a floured surface and roll it to 1/4" thick. Cut out shapes with a donut cutter. Place the donuts 1" apart on a lightly greased cookie sheet.

4. Bake at 350° for 35-40 minutes, until lightly browned. Remove from cookie sheet to cool. Store in refrigerator in a sealed container for up to 3 weeks, or in freezer for up to 3 months.

LOVE BITES

Sweet hearts for your canine sweetheart!
Makes 50.

Ingredients:
> 2-1/2 c. whole-wheat flour
> 1 c. rolled oats
> 1/4 c. wheat germ
> 2 tsp. baking powder
> 1/2 c. water
> 1 tbsp. honey or maple syrup
> 2 tbsp. canola oil
> 2 tsp. cinnamon
> 1/2 tsp. nutmeg
> 2 small (or 1 large) ripe bananas

Directions

1. Mix the dry ingredients in a large bowl. Stir in the wet ingredients and mix well (dough will be stiff).

2. Place the dough on a lightly floured surface and roll to 1/4" thick. Cut out hearts with a cookie cutter and place on a lightly greased cookie sheet.

3. Bake at 325° for 30 minutes or until hard. Remove to cool. Store in a sealed container in the refrigerator up to 3 weeks or in the freezer for up to 3 months.

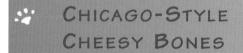 CHICAGO-STYLE CHEESY BONES

For the cheese-lover, these bones are sure to please!
Makes 25 bones.

Ingredients:
> 3 c. whole-wheat flour
> 1/2 c. wheat germ or cornmeal
> 1 c. Parmesan cheese
> 1 c. shredded cheddar cheese
> 1 tsp. dried oregano
> 2 tsp. garlic powder
> 1 tbsp. fresh or dried minced parsley
> 4 tbsp. canola (or vegetable) oil
> 1/2 c. low sodium chicken or beef broth or 1 cube of bouillon dissolved in 1/2 c. hot water.
> 2 eggs

Topping: 1/4 c. rolled oats
> 1 tsp. fresh or dried parsley

Directions

1. Mix the dry ingredients together in a large bowl. Set aside.

2. Add wet ingredients and mix (dough will be stiff). Press or roll the dough mixture out to a 1/4" thickness on a floured surface.

3. Cut out bone shapes, using a small 3-1/2" bone cookie cutter. Mix the topping ingredients together on a small, flat plate. Press the top of each bone onto the mixture and place onto a lightly greased cookie sheet.

4. Bake at 325° for 30-35 minutes or until hard. Remove and place on a rack to cool. Store in refrigerator in a sealed container for up to 3 weeks or in freezer for up to 3 months.

Optional: Cut in small fish or heart shapes for your kitty; omit topping and reduce baking time as needed.

MEATY TREAT-BALLS

Mama-mia! Makes 25 meatballs fit for your favorite animal friend!

Ingredients:
- 1/2 lb. ground turkey, beef or lamb
- 1/4 c. cornmeal
- 1/2 c. breadcrumbs
- 2 tbsp. Parmesan cheese
- 1 tsp. garlic powder
- 1/2 tsp. basil
- 1 tbsp. parsley

Coating: 1/2 c. breadcrumbs

Directions
1. Mix ingredients well. Form into 1" balls.

2. Place remaining breadcrumbs in a small bowl; add three to four balls at a time to the bowl and shake or roll around to coat.

3. Place the meatballs on a lightly greased baking pan, 1/2" apart. Bake at 325° for 15 minutes. Turn balls over and bake an additional 10 minutes. Turn the oven off. Let balls sit in the oven for an additional 20 minutes to finish cooking. Remove and cool on rack for 10-15 minutes. Keep refrigerated up to 5 days or frozen up to 2 months.

Optional: Make smaller sized meatballs for your feline friend; omit additional 10 minutes of baking time.

BLOOMIN' HOT DOG TREATS

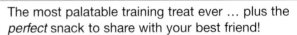

The most palatable training treat ever … plus the *perfect* snack to share with your best friend!

Ingredients
- 1 package of regular hot dogs
- Paper towels
- Microwaveable plate

Directions
1. Slice a package of eight regular hot dogs into 1/8" slices.

2. Place 2 paper towels on a circular microwaveable plate. Arrange the hot dog slices evenly on top of the covered plate. Place an additional paper towel on top of the slices.

3. Microwave on high for 8 minutes. Check slices and move those that are still soft to the outer edges of the plate. Continue microwaving on high, as follows:
> 7 minutes for training treats that are still slightly soft.
> 21 minutes for crunchy hot dog chips.

Keep refrigerated up to 1 week or frozen up to 2 months. Makes 100-125 slices.

LOVE THAT LIVER 🐾 BROWNIES

For a lip smacking, tail wagging—or purring—treat! Makes 200 cubes.

Ingredients:
 1 lb. beef or chicken livers
 2 eggs
 1/2 c. water
 1 tsp. garlic powder
 2-1/2 c. whole-wheat flour
 1 c. cornmeal

Directions:

1. Cut up raw liver and place in a blender or food processor. Add the water and chop.

2. Add the eggs and blend until mixed together.

3. Pour into a medium-sized bowl. Add the remaining ingredients and mix well.

4. Spread evenly into a lightly greased 9" x 13" pan. Bake at 350° for 30 minutes until dry but not crispy.

5. Let cool for 20 minutes. Cut into 1/2" cubes. Keep refrigerated for up to 3 days, or frozen for up to 2 months.

Optional: For "birthday cake," spread evenly in two 9" round, lightly greased cake pans. Bake until dry but not crispy. Cool 20 minutes and remove from pan. Cool an additional 20 minutes. Make frosting (see Frostings, page 70). Spread frosting on one layer; top with the second layer. Frost the top and sides of the cake.

🐾 14 CARROT APPLE 🐾 BIRTHDAY CAKE

Ingredients:
 1-1/2 c. flour
 1 c. wheat germ
 1 tsp. baking soda
 1-1/2 tsp. cinnamon
 1-1/2 c. grated fresh carrots
 1/2 c. unsweetened applesauce
 1 egg
 1/4 c. honey, molasses, or maple syrup
 3 tbsp. oil
 1 c. liquid (water, milk, or powdered milk
  mixed with water)

Directions

1. Combine dry ingredients and carrots in a medium-size bowl.

2. Beat the egg. Add the sweetener, oil, and liquid and mix well. Add to the dry ingredients and mix together.

3. Pour into a lightly greased 9" cake pan and bake at 350° for 30-35 minutes, or until cake tester comes out clean. Let cool completely before frosting.

Note: Keep frosted cake refrigerated!

Frostings

Cream cheese frosting: Mix 1/4 c. milk or water with a softened 8 oz. package of cream cheese. If necessary, add a bit more liquid, a few drops at a time, until the frosting is a smooth, spreading consistency.

Peanut butter frosting: Mix 1/4 c. milk or water with 1 c. of smooth peanut butter. If necessary, add a bit more liquid, a few drops at a time, until the frosting is a smooth, spreading consistency.

Make a candleholder by carefully scraping a hole in the center of a dog biscuit. Place on the frosted cake, with a candle in the center.

Creative Options:

• Stick baby carrots into the top of the cake, instead of candles.

• Cut out a paw print or dog bone stencil. Place the stencil on the top of the cake. Dust on ground up oats, wheat germ, or instant mashed potato flakes.

• Brush the cooled cake with chicken or beef broth. Roll the cake in wheat germ.

• Create bone "icing" by piping a line and two dots of frosting on either end to create a bone shape.

• Cut the cake into a bone shape; squeeze the scraps into a rope shape and cut into sections to serve for "second helpings."

• Press dog biscuits onto the sides of the frosted cake.

• Add a few drops of natural food coloring or spinach or beet powder for colorful frosting.

• Mix unsweetened, non-dairy carob powder with water and drizzle onto the top of the cake.

• Make the cake ahead of time and freeze without frosting. Decorate the defrosted cake right before the party.

FROZEN YOGURT CUPS

1 carton of plain or vanilla yogurt
Ice cube tray, small waxed paper cups, or molds

 Fill ice trays, cups or molds with the yogurt. Freeze until solid. Warm in a pan of warm water for 3 minutes to un-mold. Serve in bowls with the Birthday Cake slices.

(Photo permission In Focus Imagery, Jeff Green)

  THE CAT AND DOG LOVER'S IDEA BOOK

TASTY SEAFOOD NIBBLES

Ingredients:

One 6 oz. can of tuna or salmon in oil
or water (if using salmon, remove the
bones)

One 4 oz. package of cream cheese,
softened

1 tsp. low-sodium granulated chicken or
beef bouillon

3/4 c. plain, dried bread crumbs

Crushed catnip (for cats) or dried
parsley (for dogs)

Directions:

1. Drain the fish.

2. Mix the bouillon into the cream cheese until it dissolves.

3. Mix tuna or salmon and the breadcrumbs with the cream cheese mixture. Form into 1/2" balls. Roll in crushed catnip or dried parsley.

Makes 3 dozens treats. Store refrigerated up to 5 days, frozen up to 3 weeks.

Creative Options:

• Create a kitty birthday cake: Line a small container, bowl or mold with plastic wrap or waxed paper.

• Brush with a light coat of oil. Push the tuna/cream cheese mixture into the container and chill. Remove from the container, bowl or mold and gently peel the plastic or waxed paper off the "cake." Press crushed catnip over the cake to decorate.

• Add 1/8 cup of Parmesan cheese and 1-2 tbsp. of liquid broth to the mixture instead of the granulated bouillon.

• Mix 2 oz. of cream cheese with one small jar of baby food meat, instead of the tuna.

• Roll balls in Parmesan cheese instead of, or in addition to, the parsley or catnip.

Food Bowls

Note: Follow manufacturer's instructions to heat-set paints or markers for permanency. Hand wash only with mild dishwashing liquid and a soft cloth or sponge. Do not scrub or use abrasive cleanser.

2 white ceramic food bowls for each pet * (prepared per General Instructions on page 6)
Curable ceramic or glass paint **
Non-toxic polyurethane varnish that can be heated ***
Transfer paper ****
Paint brushes *****

* Design Works
** Apple Barrel Colors Indoor Outdoor Gloss (Plaid Enterprises) in the following colors:
For cat project: 20662 Black, 20631 Pink Blush, 20629 Raspberry, 20624 Dolphin, and 20352 Real Denim
For dog project: 20665 Mocha, 20647 Crown Gold, 20662 Black
*** Folk Art Outdoor Gloss Sealant (Plaid Enterprises)
**** Transfer paper (Saral Paper Corp.)
***** Flat Scrubber and Shader

(Photo courtesy Candy Kiiskila)

Cat version

1. Trace a mouse (use template on page 111) onto the bowl, using the transfer paper. Paint the mouse in the darker gray. Add lighter gray highlights. Outline in black, blending and shading. Add a black tail, eyes, nose and whiskers. Color the ears with lighter pink, shading with darker pink. Let dry. Repeat steps for each mouse, varying the angle of each. (Tip: Trace and paint one mouse at a time.)

2. Paint footprints by dipping the handle end of one of the paintbrushes into the light pink or light gray paint and adding dots to the bowl in a paw print shape.

Dog version

1. With the black paint, draw free form paw prints over the outside surface of the entire bowl, bleeding the image off the edges as shown. Paint a black circle in the center of each of the pad shapes. Let dry.

2. Paint inside each pad with either brown or gold, alternating colors as you work around the bowl.

To finish:

Let dry completely. Cure per manufacturer's instructions. Seal the painted areas of the bowl with 2-3 coats of gloss sealant to make the design more permanent. Let dry completely.

Creative Options:

- Paint cat or dog faces (pages 110-111) on the bowl, varying expressions, color and markings.

- Paint abstract, freeform bones, fish shapes, hearts, etc. onto the bowls.

- Personalize the bowls with your pet's name.

Food Mats

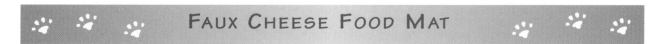

FAUX CHEESE FOOD MAT

Artist's grade or heavy-duty canvas (14" x 24" rectangle)
Paint glazes *
Paintbrush **
Light tan acrylic paint ***
Brayer with sponge roller
3" x 6" scrap of craft foam and press-on adhesive **** or permanent foam glue *****
Scissors, masking tape, foam plate
Scrap blocks of wood, plastic lids, small box lids or other suitable items to mount stamps on
Stamping sponges

* Decorator Glazes (Plaid): 53007 Lemon Yellow, 53059 Banana, 53052 Mango, 53002 New Gold Leaf
** #4 Shader (Plaid)
*** Folk Art Acrylic Paint (Plaid) 825 Taffy
**** Peel n Stick Double Sided Adhesive Sheet (Therm O Web)
***** CraftFoam Glue (Beacon Chemical Co.)

1. Iron creases on the canvas. Secure to a flat hard surface with small rolled pieces of tape placed close to the edges and underneath the canvas.

2. Squeeze Lemon Yellow and Banana glaze and Taffy acrylic paint onto a foam plate. Roll the brayer over the paint and glaze, picking up a random mixture. Roll the mixture over the entire canvas, randomly blending colors. Let dry completely.

3. Create "hole" stamps by tracing 1", 1-1/2" and 2-1/2" circles onto craft foam per instructions on page 6. Apply Mango glaze directly to one circle. Stamp the circle onto the canvas mat. Repeat this image several times, re-applying the glaze each time. Repeat this step with all three image sizes to create a random pattern over the entire mat. Let dry completely.

4. On the left side of each circle, paint a very thin crescent shape using New Gold Leaf. Vary the crescent thickness as you go. Let dry.

5. Gently sponge and wipe Mango onto the outer edges of the mat, blending the glaze into the painted mat so no harsh edges appear. (Note: Keep the mat taped down until completely dry.)

6. Turn mat upside down and secure with tape, as in Step 1. Repeat Step 2 on the WS of the mat. Let dry.

DOG BONE FOOD MAT

Artist's grade or heavy-duty canvas (14" x 24" rectangle)
Large sheet of paper or a grocery bag opened up flat
9" cake or pie pan or other 9" diameter round object to trace around
Acrylic paint *
Paint glazes **
Brayer with foam roller
Foam plate
Flat, square paint brushes, in 1/2" width and a #4 Shader
Transfer Paper

* Folk Art Acrylic Paint: 987 Wicker White, 989 Licorice
** Decorator Glazes (Plaid Enterprises): 53052 Mango
*** (Saral Paper Corp.)

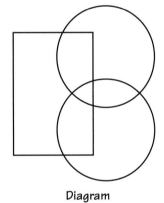

Diagram

1. Create pattern: Fold the paper in half. Draw a 6" x 12" rectangle on the paper, with one 12" side along the fold. Draw a line across the rectangle, dividing it in half into two 6" squares. Trace and draw two 9" circle shapes, side by side, overlapping the outer 12" edge, the line and each other by 1". (Diagram). Cut this half-bone shape out. Open up the pattern. Place the pattern on the canvas and cut out the bone shape.

2. Iron any creases on the canvas. Secure to a hard surface with small rolled pieces of tape placed close to the edges and underneath the canvas.

3. Squeeze white paint onto the foam plate. Roll the paint over the entire canvas bone. Let dry.

4. Paint a 1/2" wide black border around the entire outside of the shape. Let dry. Paint a free form black outline of a dog paw print in one corner of the mat and a solid black circle inside the pad portion. Let dry. Paint in the center of each shape with Mango. (Note: Keep the mat taped down until completely dry.)

5. Turn mat upside down and secure. Repeat Step 2 on the WS of the mat. Let dry.

Chapter 7

FOR DOGS ONLY/FOR CATS ONLY

For Cats Only!

Cat show trivia:
The first cat show was held in the Crystal Palace in London, England on July 13, 1871; the first United States cat show was held at Madison Square Garden in New York in 1895. Today the prestigious International Cat Show is still held there. The Supreme Cat Show is the top show held in the United Kingdom.

At Home— or Abroad?

While most municipalities forbid dogs at large, the decision to keep a cat exclusively indoors or allow it outdoors to roam is personal, but is often a subject of controversy. Keep in mind that domestic cats that regularly roam are subject to being run over by cars; killed by coyotes, territorial dogs or other wild animals; drinking contaminat-

Every individual cat should be trained based on its own natural preferences and abilities. Recently, many people have become involved in both pedigree and non-pedigree cat shows, where they can gain titles for their cats and spend a day or a weekend with other cat lovers and breeders, as well as help their pets become accustomed to changes and new people, and gain social skills.
(Photo permission Barb Zurawski)

ed water containing pesticides or puddles of anti-freeze; ingesting poisoned or sick vermin; being involved in cat fights; picking up infectious diseases, such as Feline Leukemia (FeLV), from other strange, or feral cats; being stolen; unwanted pregnancies for non-spayed queens; and injuries and accidents from broken glass, metal, etc.

(Photo courtesy Candy Kiiskila)

Litterbox Training

Litterboxes should be cleaned daily, as well as being completely emptied and thoroughly cleaned at least once a week, using cleaning products that do not contain ammonia. Adding an additional litterbox can help avoid conflicts in a multiple cat household. Allow at least one box per two to three cats, although you may need as many as one box per cat or per floor. Litterboxes range from open, plastic pans to covered, automatic, self-cleaning appliances. Some cats prefer an uncovered litterbox; others prefer more privacy. Litter also varies from clay or clumping litters to alternative fillers made from absorbent recyclable materials. The type, texture, and scent of litter may also make a big difference for more finicky cats. A cat mat will help cut down on your cat tracking filler into areas outside the litterbox.

Confining a new kitty to a small area of the house for a few days with the litterbox will help her know where it is located. Take your kitten to the box after meals and naps for the first few days. Praise her when she uses the box. If your kitty has an accident, do not act angry or rub your cat's face in it. Just clean it up. If it is solid waste, transfer it to the litterbox so the kitty will find it there and associate it with the box. Change the "accident" area into an eating area, or sprinkle the area with catnip and place a scratching post or toys there to discourage her from using the area again as a bathroom. Your cat will only be confused if you reward her with food for proper litterbox use, since cats do not want to eliminate in eating areas.

To avoid litterbox problems:

- Keep the box and litter clean.

- Keep the box in a quiet, easily accessible place away from the eating and drinking area.

- Do not move the box suddenly to a different area; move the litterbox a few inches each day, until it is in the desired spot.

- Do not scold or place undue stress on a cat near his litterbox area.

- Limit the number of cats in the household, or have enough boxes for the number of cats in your household and floors in your house.

- Use the litter your cat prefers.

- Neuter or spay your cat.

If the problem continues, determine if there have been any new stresses for your kitty or if there is a physiological reason for the accidents, such as diabetes or a urinary tract infection. Both adolescent males and females mark territory. The only way to prevent or curtail this is to neuter or spay your pet before they develop this unpleasant behavior.

Keep tracked litter to a minimum by placing your litterbox on a wood framed cork bulletin board. Stamp paw prints on the cork using permanent ink. The cork will "hold" the litter your cat tracks out of the box. Add a decorated foam core, corrugated cardboard or lightweight wood privacy screen. Some ideas for covering the screen include: Cover ing the fabric or decorating with glued or press-on adhesive cut outs from magazines, fabric or wrapping paper. If you prefer, stamp or stencil a faux garden scene or an ivy-covered wall, or paint a simple cat silhouette. For another look, cut or hand-tear tissue or decorative printed or textured paper into small "mosaic tiles" and glue them onto the screen in a colorful or subdued contemporary pattern. Cover with a light coat of sealant, if desired. Create an adjustable wooden frame by cutting two wood 1' x 2" to the length just inside the wood frame of the bulletin board. Drill holes through both pieces of wood, 1" from either end, and insert a screw and a wing or butterfly nut. Slip the decorated screen between both pieces of wood and tighten to hold; or simply mount the 1' x 2"s onto either side along the base of the screen, using tacky craft or wood glue. If desired, glue or screw the privacy screen in place onto the cork "floor" for more stability.

(Photo courtesy Dee Coleman)

Scratching

A scratching post should always be placed in the area of the house where the cat spends most of her time and away from the litter box. Scratching posts should consist of a long scratching surface that is covered with rough, tough textures such as industrial grade rougher textured carpeting, sisal, or just plain wood that has been roughed up a bit. Some cats prefer long strips of corrugated cardboard, tree stumps with the bark intact or sisal covered poles, including those found in basements. (Photo permission Barb Zurawski)

All cats have an instinctive need to scratch, much as a dog instinctively needs to chew. Cats use their sharp claws for hunting, climbing, protection and marking. Scratching keeps a cat's claws in shape by removing the dead outer sheath layer from its front claws, much like a snake sheds its skin. Scratching also indicates power by marking the item that is being scratched, as well as just being a pleasant stretching exercise. Your cat will need to learn which items she will be allowed to use for scratching, and which items she is to avoid. A scratching post, tree or toy provides your pet with a suitable scratching surface to use instead of the drapes or furniture.

At first, keep your pet and the scratching post in one room or area, preferably without furniture or draperies and away from the litterbox. Reward your kitty with positive reinforcement in the form of praise, treats, petting or play, *immediately* after each time she uses the scratching post. Teach her to associate a word, such as "post" with the act of scratching on it. When she is using the scratching post consistently, allow her into another room with furniture or drapes, and move the scratching post into this room. If she starts clawing the wrong thing, say "No" in a firm voice and then say the word you have chosen to associate with the post. If she stops, praise her. If she starts to use the post instead, praise her and reward her. Rubbing catnip on the post can attract your cat to it and help her associate the post with pleasant sensations.

If she continues to claw furniture or draperies, you will need to teach her to associate those objects with unpleasant sensations. Startle her by squirting water from a squirt bottle, squeezing a bulb bicycle horn, or using a shake can each time you witness your cat using the furniture or drapes. However, in order for any of these startle techniques to work, you must use them *only while your cat is clawing something you don't want her to*. Each time she stops, praise her and use the word for the post, praising her again when she uses it. If you are not going to be present, you will have to make the undesirable objects unpleasant for her to touch. This can be accomplished by covering the furniture or drapes with an electric mat, sticky double-sided tape, aluminum foil, molded chicken wire, plastic bubble wrap, or a plastic carpet runner (with the nubs up). Another option is to scent wood furniture with a fragrance that cats do not like, such as eucalyptus, lemon, cinnamon, or Bitter Apple. If you have a kitten, get her used to having her claws clipped. Often, by simply keeping claws trimmed you can effectively reduce the damage and some of the instinct to scratch. You can also place special plastic claw caps on the claws.

MOUSE SCRATCHER

This scratching aid can be used either on the floor or hanging from a doorknob.

Sheet of heavy corrugated cardboard or foam core board
Fishing line
Industrial, low pile carpet
Sisal rope
Hammer punch, or other heavy-duty punch
Pencil, jumbo paper clips
Fast grab, heavy-duty non-toxic tacky craft *, wood, or fabric glue
Leather shoelace
Scrap of pink felt
Two 1/2" and one 1" black pompoms

*Gem-Tac (Beacon Chemical Co.)

1. Enlarge and trace the mouse pattern from page 109. Cut out 2 shapes from the carpet and 1 from the cardboard or foam core board. Mark a RS on the cardboard/foam core board. Mark and poke A, B, C and D Holes through the cardboard/foam core board, as shown on the Diagram. Make a matching Hole A in one of the carpet pieces.

Diagram

2. Cut 1 yard of fish line. Fold in half to double. Insert both ends through the carpet's Hole A from the RS to the WS and then insert the line through Hole A from the RS of the foam core/cardboard. With the fish line now on the WS of the foam core/cardboard, separate the two ends and insert one end through B and the other through C, coming up onto the RS of the cardboard/foam core board. Tie the ends together. (Pull loop out and make sure it is not glued inside the carpet in Step 5 so it can be used for a hanger.)

3. Cut an 18" piece of sisal. Using the hammer punch, make a matching D hole through both pieces of the carpet, large enough for the sisal to slide through. Glue both pieces of the carpet to the board, clipping with paper clips to keep the edges together. Lay flat and place heavy books on top until completely dry (overnight). Insert the sisal into hole D, through all the layers and knot it at both ends.

4. Glue additional sisal around the edges, using paper clips again to hold it in place as you go until dry.

5. Cut three 4" long pieces from the leather shoelace. Hold the 3 pieces together and tie in the middle with a small piece of fish line. Trim fish line. Glue onto carpet front for whiskers, as shown. Cut 2 pink ears (use enlarged pattern piece, page 111) from the felt. Glue ears and 2 pompom eyes as shown. Glue a pompom nose over the tied center of the whiskers.

by Bernard Danenberg

One 3/4" x 8" x 24" long piece of plywood or wood shelving (A)
One 1-1/2" x 1-1/2" x 8" long piece of wood (B)
(Note: The thickness of the wood can vary depending on how much slope is desired)
8" wide x 30" long strip of low pile, industrial grade carpet, with the ribs of the carpet running lengthwise.
Acrylic paint in your choice of color and a paintbrush
Electric staple gun
Wood glue
Medium grade sandpaper
Optional: Self-stick, screw or nail-on plastic, or rubber furniture protectors.
Screws

1. Using glue or screws, attach piece A along one of the short edges of piece B, 1" from the edge. Paint and let dry. (See Diagram.)

2. Sand any rough edges on the wood and paint all surfaces. Let dry completely.

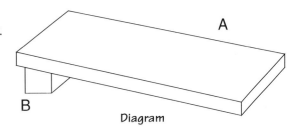
Diagram

3. Wrap the end of the carpet strip around the short edge on piece A, butting up against piece B. Staple in place. Holding the carpet taut, wrap it over the edges of piece A and staple in place. If desired, glue the long edges to secure.

Optional: Add furniture protectors underneath piece B to protect floor surface.

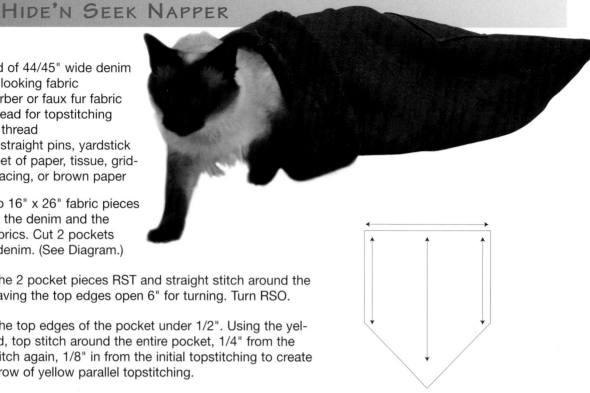

1-1/4 yard of 44/45" wide denim or similar looking fabric
1 yard Berber or faux fur fabric
Yellow thread for topstitching
Matching thread
Scissors, straight pins, yardstick
Large sheet of paper, tissue, gridded interfacing, or brown paper

1. Cut two 16" x 26" fabric pieces from both the denim and the Berber fabrics. Cut 2 pockets from the denim. (See Diagram.)

2. Place the 2 pocket pieces RST and straight stitch around the edges, leaving the top edges open 6" for turning. Turn RSO.

3. Press the top edges of the pocket under 1/2". Using the yellow thread, top stitch around the entire pocket, 1/4" from the edges. Stitch again, 1/8" in from the initial topstitching to create a double row of yellow parallel topstitching.

4. Change thread to match the denim. Place the pocket, centered, onto the RS of one of the denim pieces, with the point of the pocket 3" above the 16" bottom edge. Leaving the top edge of the pocket open, stitch around the sides and bottom of the pocket, 1/8" in from the initial row of topstitching.

Diagram

5. Place the denim pieces RST and straight stitch along the 2 sides and bottom edges, leaving the top edge open. Repeat with the Berber pieces, trimming the corners and turning RSO. (Do not turn the denim RSO.)

6. Place the Berber "sack" inside of the denim "sack," matching side seams, and with the fabrics RST. Pin in place along the unstitched top edges. Stitch the top edges together, leaving 6" open to turn. Turn RSO. Hand-sew the opening shut and fold the top edge down to form a cuff.

Creative Options

• Use a luxurious non-metallic, non-snagging material such as velvet or velour instead of Berber and denim.

• Use lightweight woven cotton fabric, with a sheet of paper sandwiched in between the layers or use a stiff lining fabric; your cat will love the crinkly sound!

• Appliqué a cat face or silhouette (see patterns, page 111) onto the denim sack instead of the pocket; or sew the image onto the pocket.

Decorate a simple cardboard carton to create a cat playhouse with a cutout door and optional windows. Stamp a brick or stone pattern or paint on trees, vines and flowers or decorate the box to resemble your own home. Be creative by painting a more humorous playhouse, such as a fish tank or a birdcage, or paint a mouse hole or two with mice peeking out. Paint the house to resemble Swiss cheese (see page 72 for cat food mat) for a real surprise! Use a sturdy carton, approximately 16" high x 18" wide x 12" deep (larger for a multiple cat household) and add a carpet mat inside, if desired. Create the house shown in the photo by cutting or tearing a kitchen sponge into several irregularly shaped rectangular "stones," each in a correspondingly different size. Apply non-toxic paint or glaze directly to the sponge stamp and stamp "stones" over the side of a pre-painted carton with the doorway cut-out, varying sizes, angles and paint color combinations as you go. Shown: (Plaid Enterprises) Folk Art Acrylic 879 Linen and Decorator Glazes 53052 Mango, 53003 Silver Leaf, 53034 Black, 53006 White, 53011 Russet.

For Dogs Only!

The Educated Dog

Prevent problem behaviors by teaching basic commands when your puppy is small. Although a seven-week old puppy is capable of learning to sit and come when called, remember that you are working with a baby and keep the training sessions very short. Always use a kind voice and a gentle touch when training your puppy, using a sterner sounding voice only when your puppy really misbehaves. Using a loud, angry sounding voice or rough hands will only frighten your puppy. The idea is to teach your puppy the right things to do instead of just saying "No" or punishing him each time he does something that you don't like. If you use positive reinforcement (see page 17), coupled with pleasant associations, your puppy will not only *learn* the right things to do, but soon *prefer* doing the right things instead of the wrong things.

Participating in dog obedience classes will help socialize and teach the dog, as well as help you become more knowledgeable about canine behavior and avoid many of the pitfalls that can arise as your puppy grows up. Adult, rescue, and shelter dogs can also benefit from attending classes. Doing something together will cement the bond between you and your pet and introduce you to some of the performance events and sports activities available in most areas of the country throughout the year. Training and competing for titles, ribbons, and prizes is an additional way to have fun with your dog, as well as meet other dog lovers. There are many people who start out attending a basic obedience class just to have a well-behaved pet and wind up becoming involved in one or more dog sports for a lifetime of enjoyment.

Confirmation or Breed shows are the canine counterpart of the cat shows. By process of elimination, trained judges determine the one animal in each recognized breed that most closely typifies each individual breed standard. In dog shows, the winner in each breed is awarded points and "Best of Breed" (BOB). Next, all the BOB dogs are judged against each other within their "Groups." In AKC there are seven "Groups" (Herding, Working, Non-Sporting, Sporting, Toy, Terrier, Hound). Each "Group" will have one dog that is chosen "Best in Group." These seven semi-finalists then compete for the prestigious "Best in Show," the winner of the dog show. Dogs competing in confirmation eventually gain the title of "Champion" (CH).

A.

Another popular competitive sport is *Obedience*. Titles from the first level on up include CD (Companion Dog), CDX (Companion Dog Excellent), UD (Utility Dog), UDX (Utility Dog Excellent) and OTCH (Obedience Titled Champion). Each level of competition involves increasingly complex and challenging exercises, which the handler and dog must perform as perfectly as possible. Every dog/handler team begins with 200 points. During their performance, the judge evaluates how they have executed each exercise, and deducts 1/2 to several points for minor or major handler or dog errors (sitting crooked, lagging behind during off-leash heeling, etc.). Certain errors, as well as too many points deducted, can result in an "NQ" (Not Qualifying) score, for which the team gets no credit from that show towards their title.

Agility is one of the fastest growing dog sports. Here, dogs and handlers run through different courses in which the dogs must go through, under or over a series of obstacles (including hurdles, tunnels, tires, A-frames, weave poles, and others) in a certain order. There are also decoy obstacles included on the course

OESCA 6 12 1986

FOURTH
PLACE
NOVICE B

B.

C.

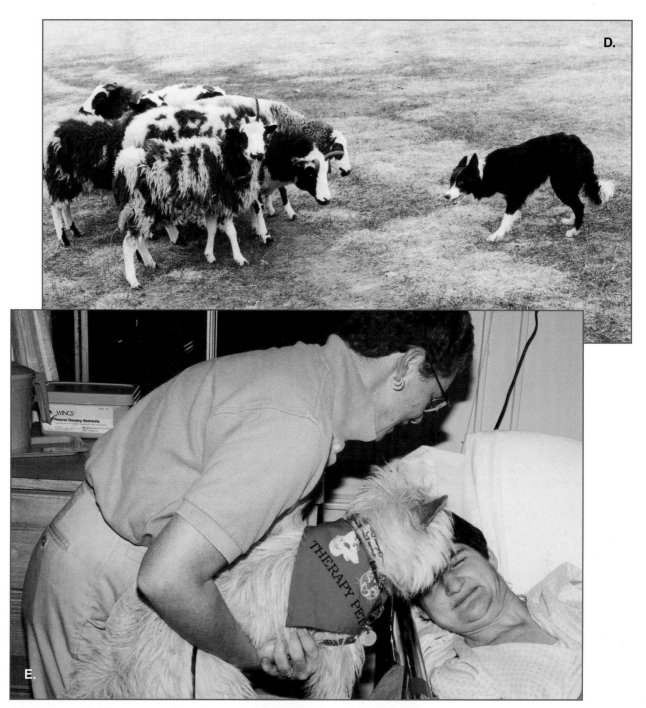

There are several different types of competitive events, trials and testing that dog owners can compete in. Some of these choices include All-breed and Specialty Shows and Junior Showmanship (A, page 83), Obedience competitions (B, page 84), Agility Events (C, page 84), Herding Tests and Trials (D), as well as Lure Coursing, Flyball, and various Field Tracking, and Earthdog Trials. Other non-competitive activities include simple Good Canine Citizen Testing as well as serving in a Therapy Dog group (E). Information on these different areas of service, competition and training can be found through the various registries (see page 112), magazines or training facilities throughout the country. (Photos courtesy of and permission by: A, D, Pat Schulz; B, Judy Roth; C In Focus Imagery, ; E- Peggy Farrell-Kidd)

that dogs are supposed to ignore. The dog, therefore, must take its cues from the handler in order to know which obstacles to approach and when. Since the course is set up differently for each trial, the handlers must pre-walk the course just prior to the competition to understand the order and path they must get the dog to take. The teams are judged against a scoring system (with points taken against faults) as well as time. Dogs can also "NQ" if they refuse an obstacle, go "off-course," have a time fault or too many errors. Agility also includes different courses and levels of competition, with different titles to be earned.

Basic Obedience Training For Dogs

Obedience training is a wonderful way to bond with your pet, as well as avoiding destructive animal behavioral problems.
(Photo courtesy Maureen Tobias and Pat Schulz)

Every dog should be taught the five basic commands: *Sit, Down, Stay, Come,* and *Heel*, as well as some additional ones, such as *Leave it* (see "Chewing," page 31) or *Off* (See "Dominance/Aggression, page 32). All these commands should initially be taught on leash in a quiet area and preferably when the puppy is well rested and has had a chance to eliminate immediately prior to the training session. There are several positive methods of teaching basic commands, including clicker training, food motivation, and verbal praise. The following exercises combine verbal praise and food motivation, which can be used on puppies or dogs that are at least somewhat food-driven. Food is only used as a motivational tool, until the animal begins to respond to the verbal command automatically on a regular basis. At that point, begin weaning your pet off the food by offering her food as praise every other time. If desired, you can also begin to substitute other pleasurable rewards, such as petting, or playing after obeying a command or a string of commands. Continue to reduce the food offerings until she no longer needs the treats to obey the command. Verbal praise, in a happy, loving voice should always be offered when the dog obeys your command.

Obedience training can also help to save your pet's life should she ever accidentally get loose or out of the yard. Never chase your dog to catch her; she will just think it is a fun game to play and will soon learn to run *away* from you rather than to you. Instead, call her to you in a happy tone of voice and then run in the direction you want her to come. Her chase instinct will kick in and she will return to you, thinking it is fun to come to you, especially if she is then rewarded with your verbal praise and a treat. Teaching your dog to go *Down* immediately on command, however, is the safest way to stop a dog that is racing away from you. Once she has stopped, you can then call her to *"Come"* to you. Avoid using an angry tone of voice to punish her from running away after she has obeyed your command to *Come* and returned to you, or she will associate the angry tone with coming to you, instead.

Try these easy training treats:

❧ Sliced hot dogs (see Bloomin' Hot Dog treats, page 68)

❧ Small apple chunks

❧ Thin celery or carrot slices

❧ Small chunks of cheese

❧ Spread peanut butter or soft cheese on a wooden spoon, or on the fingers of your left hand, to teach heeling to a puppy or as a motivation/reward for the command "Watch!"

Teach your puppy to SIT

Sit and *Down* are taught initially with the puppy facing you. With a training treat in your hand, tell your puppy to sit while raising your hand up and slightly towards her. While she is looking up at the treat, continue to move your hand forward, leading her to sit as she follows the treat. Praise her and give her the treat only when she has sat. Continue this exercise until she sits each time you say *"Sit."*

Teach your puppy DOWN

This is similar to and follows the exercise above. Place your dog into a *Sit*. Next, you will move your hand and treat down to the ground, saying the word *"Down."* As she follows the treat, move your hand slightly toward her at the same time. This forward movement will naturally force her to move backwards while keeping her hind end lowered so that she is in a complete *Down* position. This exercise is a little more difficult for some dogs to understand and might take more time to reinforce.

Teach your puppy to STAY

(Usually used in combination with *Sit* or *Down*.) Place your puppy in front of or next to you in a *Sit* or a *Down*. Tell her to *"Stay."* Initially, a few seconds is all you can expect. Repeat the exercise, praising her in a quiet voice after just a few seconds, while she is still in the sit or down position. Next, tell her a release word, such as "Okay" or "Free." The release word tells her that the *Stay* exercise is over and that she can now move. Reinforce the exercise by repeating it several times a day and gradually extending the length of time for her to stay. Practice this exercise before she eats, when you are opening a door, or when company comes. Later, when she is able to Stay for several minutes, ask her to do a long *Sit* or *Down* while you are watching television or doing stationary chores and will be able to correct her if she breaks. If she moves before you release her, place her back in the same spot and begin the exercise again, but only for a reduced time period.

Teach your puppy to COME

Holding a treat in front of you, say the puppy's name and the word *"Come."* If she comes to you, praise her and give her the treat. Repeat this exercise several times, gradually increasing the distance between you and the puppy. Alternate with standing still and stepping backwards a few steps, saying the word *"Come"* while you are moving backwards. Never tell your puppy to *"Come"* in an angry tone of voice or after she has done something wrong to scold her. If you do, she will associate the command *Come* with unpleasantness and you will have to train her all over again, using a totally different call word.

Teach your puppy to HEEL

This exercise is best taught using a short training leash in a quiet place with few distractions. Tell your puppy to *"Sit"* next to you on your left side. Holding a treat in your left hand, say the word *"Heel"* and begin to walk forward. Hold the treat under her nose as you go, letting her lick or gently chew pieces off of it as she walks with you. Praise her and give her the treat while she is heeling next to you. In the beginning, do not expect more than a few feet at a time. Gradually, increase the distance she must walk with you before she is rewarded.

When she is consistently walking next to you, change the exercise slightly by holding a small soft treat in your left hand at shoulder height or in your mouth and telling her to *"Watch."* As soon as she looks up at you, drop the treat and say, *"Catch."* She will eventually learn to catch the treat in mid-air. Repeat this periodically during the heeling exercise in addition to saying the word *"Heel."* This *"watch"* reinforcement teaches the dog to focus on you rather than on distractions around her and, at the same time, keeps her at the correct heel position next to you.

(Photo courtesy Pat Schulz)

Keep your leashes handy for fun walks or going to training class. Decorate an unfinished wood hat or decorative rack with faux tiles made from your child's drawings. Simply mount the drawings on mat board and cover with glossy, self-adhesive laminating sheets. Paint or stain the rack and brush on sealant. When dry, attach the tiles as shown. Products used: Walnut Hollow hat rack, gel stain, Folk Art Outdoor Gloss Sealant (Plaid Enterprises), Peel N Stick Double-sided Adhesive and Gloss Finish Decorative Laminating Sheets (Therm O Web).

Creative Options:

• Use photos, magazine cutouts or drawing from the patterns on pages 109 to 111.

• Stencil or stamp paper squares.

Artwork appearing on the Faux Tile Leash Rack is by Joey Hirsch.

Digging

To prevent or eliminate digging:

Relieve stress or boredom through interactive play, adequate exercise to tire him out, and outings at dog parks or in neighborhood dog play groups.

Give your dog a job to do, such as Therapy visits or Agility training and trials.

Fill holes with rocks or cover with chicken wire.

Give your dog one isolated area in the yard that is hers for digging.

Keep Arctic dogs indoors in hot or cold weather (they instinctively dig to get warm or cool off).

Neuter or spay your pets to reduce their desire to escape under fences or gates, which often occurs with a non-spayed female in heat or a non-neutered male that detects a female in heat.

Build dig-proof fences and gates with buried chicken wire or wood, asphalt, gravel, bricks or cement all around the perimeter base of the fence.

✿ DOG TOY
✿ BOX

Decorate an unfinished wooden crate by stamping images and words as shown. First, finish the crate in a solid or faux finish of your choice. After all the stamped images are dry, seal with a couple coats of tough, non-toxic sealant. (Note: The heart, circle and bone images were stamped with stamps made per the general instructions on page 6.)

Used for the project shown: Folk Art Acrylic Paint 879 Linen and Antiquing Medium 812 Down Home Brown, 820 Apple Butter Brown; Decorator Glazes: 53033 Bark Brown, 53011 Russet, 53032 Deep Woods. All products Plaid Enterprises)

Barking

Dogs bark for many reasons. They bark to sound an alarm, announce that dad is home, warn away intruders (like a rabbit or a squirrel) or other dogs, tell you they need to go out, want to play, want to come inside, are excited or that they are just lonely. If your dog only barks when she needs to go outside for her business or to get your attention for a specific reason do not correct her behavior, since she isn't doing anything wrong. Praise her for telling you. Some barking can be helpful, especially in situations of real danger or to deter intruders. However, too much barking or barking for each and every reason listed above can become annoying to you and your neighbors.

Prevent nuisance, unnecessary or excessive barking before it becomes a habit by teaching the command "Quiet." When your pup barks, immediately hold her muzzle shut momentarily and say "Quiet" in a firm, matter-of-fact tone of voice. Avoid shouting, however, since it will only sound like you are barking, too. Let go of her muzzle. If she does not bark when you let go, praise her by repeating the command, along with your praise word ("Good dog…. *quiet!*") and offer a food reward or toss a ball (as long as that isn't the behavior that triggered the barking). If she barks when you remove your hand from her muzzle, repeat until you get five seconds of quiet so you can praise and reward her. If repeated or unnecessary barking continues, try a squirt of lemon juice in her mouth. It will force the dog's mouth to pucker, giving you the few seconds of non-barking to teach the concept and command for being quiet.

Barking habits are difficult to break, especially when inadvertently reinforced by their owners. Dogs who bark to get their way, such as wanting go out and play, will only continue if the owner lets them go out after they bark. See it from their perspective: dog in crate; dog barks; door opens. It worked! Dog in crate, dog barks to come out; crate door opens and dog comes out! Again, it worked! Now, change the scenario: dog barks, crate door opens, owner places hand on muzzle or squirts lemon juice in mouth, mouth puckers, that word "Quiet" and crate door closes and owner leaves. If the dog remains quiet for several seconds afterward, then the crate door opens, plus the dog gets praises and treats. In this scenario, your dog will learn that good things happen by being quiet. For any of these techniques to work, however, you must be consistent. If you only correct the barking once in a while, you will just confuse the dog and she will never understand what you want.

Persistent, chronic barking sometimes needs additional measures. Sound-correction units and electronic bark collars can be effective in extreme cases; these devices, however, must be used carefully and correctly to avoid harming the animal and to effectively associate the barking with the correction. It is wise to consult an expert if you feel you need to use one of these devices.

Housebreaking

One of the advantages in getting a puppy is that it is easier to mold it into the pet you want. One distinct disadvantage is that you will need to housebreak a baby who doesn't wear diapers and may not develop the ability to control his bladder for a few more weeks. A puppy can hold his bladder for the same number of hours that are equivalent to his age in months, plus one; for example: a five-month old puppy can stay in the crate for a maximum of six hours during the day before needing to relieve itself.

Dogs instinctively do not soil their dens so they must be taught to view the *entire* house as the den. In the mind of a puppy, however, his crate or a single room may be what he perceives to be the "den," with the rest of the house as "outside." While kittens will associate different rooms in the house with different activities, puppies need to be taught where you want them to eliminate. Puppies or dogs who learn to soil their crates or "inside" in neglectful or abusive homes, or in the less than desirable living conditions found in puppy mills, pet stores or animal shelters (locked in crates twenty-four hours a day), may never completely become housebroken. Certain breeds of dogs can also be more difficult to housebreak than others, and can take months before accidents no longer happen.

People who obtain a puppy or young dog often expect that animal to hold its bladder for ten to twelve hours a day. Not only is this impossible for a puppy, it is not healthy for an older dog either, and can lead to kidney or bladder problems or soiling in the house. If you have house soiling problems that do not seem correctable, first rule out physical problems with a trip to the veterinarian. Otherwise, consider consulting a behavioral specialist.

To prevent house soiling and bathroom accidents, you will first need to realize that it will take work and effort on your part. Learn to recognize the times when your puppy will need to go to the bathroom: immediately after waking or vigorous play, ten minutes after drinking or eating, and many other times in between. Watch for the telltale body language: sniffing, circling, and/or squatting. Anticipate when your puppy will need to go outside, as well as helping him to associate the act of eliminating *outside* the "den." Teach a command word or phrase to associate with the act of soiling outside, such as "Go potty," "Do your business," or "Hurry up." Use this command *each and every time you bring your puppy outside*. Repeat the command until the puppy starts to urinate or defecate. Follow that act *immediately* with a combination of a treat and a praise word or phrase in a very excited and happy tone of voice. Really ham it up so that your puppy thinks that he has just done the most wonderful thing in the entire world! If you are consistent, your puppy will eventually learn to eliminate "on command" … a very handy trait when you are running late for a doctor's appointment.

(Photo courtesy Barb Zurawski)

In addition to keeping tabs on timing, make sure to use a cover-up spray on areas where the inevitable indoor "accidents" have occurred. Most housebreaking accidents occur because the owner did not recognize the signs, pay attention, or unrealistically expected the puppy to "hold it." Also, never rub a puppy's nose in excrement or punish your puppy by scolding him *after* you find the accident. To be effective, you must catch him in the act. Say "No!" in a firm voice or clap your hands to startle and stop her from going. Then immediately pick her up and take her outside to finish. Praise her and reward her for finishing outside. This will continue to reinforce outside elimination with something good.

Naughty Puppy Cross-Stitch
(Permission Janlynn Corp.; illustration ©Gail Green)

15" x 18" piece of 14-count Aida cloth (ivory or white)

#24 tapestry needle

Skeins of 6-strand DMC Embroidery Floss in the following colors:

⌛	Medium Green	3347	·	White	000
▲	Dark Green	3345	=	Light Green	3348
⌐	Very Light Blue Violet	3747	A	Light Old Gold	676
⋒	Medium Tan	435	∾	Medium Flesh	945
°	Very Light Flesh	941	♋	Very Light Old Gold	677
⊕	Dark Salmon	3328	✳	Light Mocha Brown	3782
	Light Flesh	941	◩	Dark Tan	434
↘	Light Blue	794	V	Very Light Mocha Brown	3033
O	Light Salmon	3713	//	Light Tan	436
△	Cream	712	▫	Off-White	746
#	Dark Flesh	3773	▨	Very Dark Rust Brown	975
⋔	Medium Rust Brown	976	C	Very Light Tan	738
▨	Medium Blue	3807	◈	Dark Coffee Brown	801
⌁	Medium Salmon	760	⊕	Light Rust Brown	3827
✤	Very Dark Blue	791	■	Black	310

Notes:

• 2 skeins of embroidery floss are needed for Medium Green, White, and Light Green; all other colors listed above require one skein.

• The following stitches will be used: full cross-stitch, quarter cross-stitch, back stitch, straight stitch and French Knot.

• Work all cross-stitches and quarter cross-stitches first. Refer to the NP Symbol Legend for the number of strands used to stitch the design. Unless otherwise noted, use one strand to work all back stitches; all other stitches are worked in two strands.

• Finished size: 11" x 14".

Back Stitches

————————	Dog's eye and nose highlights (two strands)	000
————————	Portions of the dog's irises, paws and muzzle indicated by ++++ on the graph	434
++++++++++++	Dog's nose and remainder of eyes	310
————————	Tip of dog's tail	738
————————	Green hair tie indicated by • • • • on the graph	3345
————————	Girl's hair	435
– – – – – –	Doll's shoes, ribbon, eyes, and buttons	791
————————	Doll's sleeves, collar and edge of dress shirt indicated by — — — on the graph	794
• • • • • • • • • •	Doll's dress bodice and socks	3328
————————	Doll's mouth (two strands)	3328
————————	Doll's nose and hands; all flesh areas on the girl	3773
————————	Bone	3782

Straight Stitches
(Use two strands)

Grass indicated by • • • • on the graph	3345
Remainder of grass	3348

French Knots
(Indicated by small dots found on the intersecting lines of the graph. Use two strands to work French Knots.)

Dog's muzzle	801

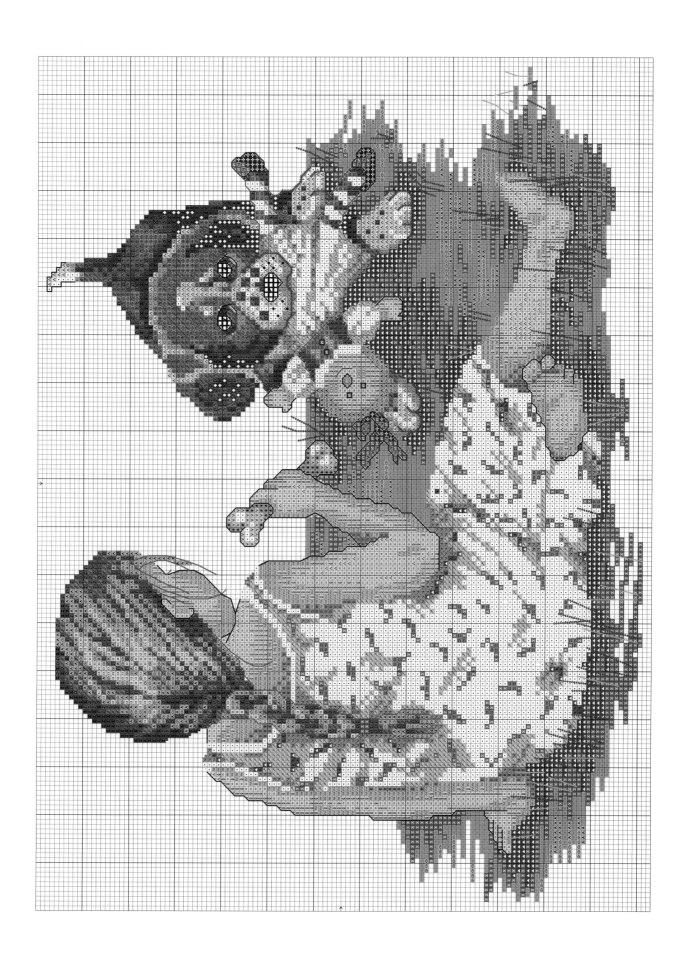

Chapter 8
CELEBRATIONS

For your dog, every birthday is like seven. Throw a fun birthday party to celebrate! (Photo permission In Focus Imagery, Jeff Green)

Birthday Bash Ideas

❧ Make canine-theme party invitations with rubber stamps or computer generated images or software.

❧ Invite well-behaved and socialized dogs from a training class or dog play group. If you are including other types of pets in the family, make sure that all invited guests are used to these types of pets.

❧ Offer your guests pre-made paper party hats or make your own by decorating plain white cone-shaped hats with bone prints, paw prints or words like "Bow-wow!" Use rubber stamps, stencils, markers or whatever medium strikes your fancy.

❧ Offer your guests one of the flavored waters as a special treat.

❧ Make simple decorated collars or bandanas for your guests to wear and take home.

❧ Take Polaroid pictures of each guest. Slip each picture into a little decorated frame to take home.

❧ Decorate goody bags or purchase "doggie bags" from a local restaurant. Fill them with some of the delicious treats on pages 65 to 70.

Note: To avoid possible fighting, do not offer rawhide or bones as a party treat or favor. Also, make sure that all dogs and treats are under adequate human supervision and control.

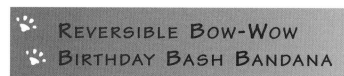

REVERSIBLE BOW-WOW
BIRTHDAY BASH BANDANA

1 yard each of 2 coordinating polyester/cotton blend woven
   fabrics (Makes 2 large, 4 medium or 6 small bandanas)
1 yard iron-on adhesive* or other bonding material
Fabric glue **

* HeatnBond Ultra Hold Iron-On Adhesive (Therm O Web)
** Gem-Tac or Fabri-Tac Permanent Adhesive (Beacon Chemical Co.)

1. Following manufacturer's instruction, bond the fabrics WST using iron-on adhesive. Create the bandana per General Instructions, page 7. Trim edges, if necessary with a pinking or straight edge scissors.

2. Cut out a bone from each contrasting fabric scrap and glue onto the appropriate side. When wearing, fold the top edge over to show the contrasting fabric.

Creative Options:

● Cut single layer bandanas for guests, using a pinking shears.

● Write each guest's name on a bandana with decorative paint, paint markers or stenciled or stamped on with fabric paint or textile ink. (Make sure all ink is heat-set and non-toxic.)

Following general instructions, make (2 large, 4 medium or 6 small) bandanas for your guests using two contrasting fabrics fused together with iron-on adhesive.*

● Use a different template from page 111. Cut out multiple smaller bone shapes, hearts, paw prints (heart and small ovals), circles for tennis balls, or silhouettes of dogs or cats. Bond a different fabric shape to each side of the bandana.

● For thicker necks, bond or sew ribbon along the long edge or 1" - 2" strips of hook and loop tape.

Play games that show off your dog training ability:

❖ Put all the guests in a long Sit or Down, Stay for five minutes. Offer treats and prizes to the guests who remain sitting or down the full five minutes.

❖ If weather permits, throw the party outside and have relay races or games of fetch for everyone.

❖ Play "doggie twister" or tic-tac-toe, using marked off "spots" on the ground.

❖ Place a few slices of hot dogs or small apple chunks in shallow, water-filled containers and allow the guests to "bob" for the treats.

❖ Play "find it" games. Invert several containers and have the dogs take turns, one at a time to find treats hidden under some of the containers.

White ceramic cake plate*, prepared per General Instructions, page 6
Paint for glass and ceramics **
Assorted paint brushes ***
Scrap of cardstock
Masking tape
Transfer paper ****
Craft knife
Optional: Non-toxic polyurethane varnish that can be heated *****

* Design Works
** Apple Barrel Colors Indoor Outdoor Gloss (Plaid Enterprises) in the following colors: 20662 Black, 20647 Crown Gold, 20663 Beachcomber Beige, 20621 White, 20352 Real Denim, 20665 Mocha
*** Round and flat scrubbers, large paint brush with a flat tipped handle
**** Saral Paper Corp.
***** Folk Art Outdoor Gloss Sealant (Plaid Enterprises)

Note: Clean the brush in between each color.

1. Trace the dog silhouette pattern from page 111 in the center of the scrap of cardstock. Cut the image out with the craft knife to create a stencil template.

2. Place the stencil template on the plate rim and secure lightly with tape. Apply the Mocha paint by pouncing paint in the open stencil area with the

round scrubber. Use short strokes to form a fur texture. Let dry. Remove the stencil template.

3. Position the stencil pattern in another spot on the rim. Repeat Step 3, pouncing with Denim or Ochre. Continue moving the stencil pattern, varying angles and colors until the entire rim is painted.

4. Using the large paintbrush, dip the tip of the handle into black paint and apply a dot on the dog for a nose. Repeat for all the dogs. Let dry. Clean off the handle. Apply Beige dots in between the dogs as shown and draw in straight lines between the dots with the flat scrubber to create bones. Let dry.

5. Again, clean off the handle. Continuing to use the tip, apply white dots for eyes on all the dogs. Let dry. Using the flat scrubber handle tip this time, carefully dot black in each dog's eye for the pupils. Let dry completely and cure, following the manufacturer's directions.

Optional: For more permanence, apply 2-3 coats of sealant to the rim.

Creative Options:

● Paint the images underneath a clear glass plate instead.

● Create two stencil patterns; use to create mirror images on the plate.

● Use the discarded cut out portion of the dog as a "mask" to cover up a painted image; position the stencil pattern slightly overlap ping the "mask" and paint as instructed. Let dry. When you remove the stencil pattern and the mask, the dogs will appear to be overlapped.

● Paint using glass or ceramic markers instead.

● Create a stencil pattern of a bone or paw print and paint these images.

Make sure to take plenty of pictures or capture the action on a video recorder. (See tips on pages 105.) (Photos permission In Focus Imagery, Jeff Green)

Dressing Up

Although some dogs and cats naturally enjoy wearing costumes or fancy collars, most have to get used to the idea that dressing up can be fun. Use the same positive reinforcement techniques on page 30. Begin with very short sessions and expect only a few seconds tolerating the item, at first. Verbally praise your pet each time he keeps the item on without trying to remove it. Focus his attention on a treat as you gently put the item on him to help him associate dress-up with something pleasant. Repeat this several times a day if possible. Gradually extend the time your pet wears the item, but always stay within his tolerance level. Pets that have been exposed to dressing up as puppies or kittens adapt more easily than an older pet, but a lot of patience can pay off and lead to fun for you and your pet.

(Photo courtesy In Focus Imagery, Jeff Green)

KITTY BERET

For the Kitty Beret, cut a 10" circle from felt. Fold the edges under 1/2" to form a casing and stitch, leaving a 1" opening. Insert a 12" piece of 1/8" elastic into the casing. Stitch the ends of the elastic together. Hand-stitch the opening shut. Cut a 2" long 1/4" wide strip of felt. Form a loop and hand tack in the center of the beret.

1 yard each of yellow and orange felt *
1/4 yard each of bright pink, green and blue felt *
2 pieces of 14 gauge wire in the following lengths: 46" and 54"
Hot glue
8" strip of hook and loop tape
Wire cutters
Thread to match
Optional: 1 to 2 yards of 3/8" wide elastic
Child's narrow headband and 1 straight chenille stem (medium to large dogs) or one curly chenille stem (all size dogs and cats) **
Two 1" or 1-1/2" multi-colored pompoms **

* Yellow, Mango Tango, Pink Mist, Wave Green, and Limbo Lime Rainbow Classic Felt (Kunin)
** Fibre-Craft

Directions

1. Measure around your pet's ribcage. Add (5", 6", 7") to this measurement for the length. Cut an orange strip of felt the length by 8" wide (piece A). Cut a second orange strip 2" x 14" (piece B).

2. Cut 4 pieces of yellow felt, using the teardrop mouse pattern, (enlarged to the same size as the scratching mouse pattern), cutting the bottom of the piece along the line indicated on the pattern.

3. Place 2 of the yellow pieces of felt together. Glue or straight-stitch around the curved edge, leaving the straight edge open. Repeat for the remaining pair. Turn both wing pieces RSO. Top stitch around the curve, 1/2" in from the edge.

4. Insert the 54"piece of wire into one wing, then the other, creating a figure 8 shape (piece C). (See Diagram A.) Cut the wire, leaving an additional 2" of wire sticking out from each end of the wing pair. Twist the wire ends together. Hand-sew the straight open ends of the wing together so the wire doesn't show.

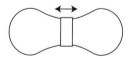

Diagram A

5. Cut an additional 4 pieces of yellow felt, 1/2" smaller than the first 4 pieces. Repeat Steps 3 and 4 to create a second, smaller figure 8-shaped wing, using the 46" piece of wire (piece D).

6. Cut circles, ovals or other shapes, if desired, in various sizes and color combinations to decorate the wings. Glue on each section as desired.

(Photo permission In Focus Imagery, Jeff Green)

7. Fold piece A in half lengthwise and stitch along the long end. Turn RSO, positioning so the seam is centered **(Diagram B)**. Fold the short ends under 1/2" and stitch across. Sew 2 parallel 4" strips of hook and loop tape to the 2 short ends on piece A, as shown in the Diagram.

Diagram B

8. Place the smaller wings under the larger wings in a staggered position so that the smaller ones are still visible and the center of the two pieces measures 5". Hand-tack the two sets of wings together securely across the center.

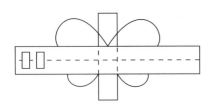

Diagram C

9. Place piece A, RS up and centered, underneath the wings **(Diagram C)**. Glue or hand-stitch the wings to the center of piece A, using two parallel rows of stitching to make it secure. Wrap piece B on top and around the wings' center and glue or hand-stitch underneath.

Creative Options:

● Create bumblebee wings and antenna set using black and yellow colors. Add black stripes to piece A.

● Create an angel set, using white felt. Glue sparkly glitter onto the wings and antenna.

● Make the antennae only and give them to birthday party guests. Have a contest to see which animal keeps his on the longest—make sure to take plenty of photos.

● Glue different lightweight items on a headband, such as fabric-covered Styrofoam cut into the shape of rabbit ears (see photo on page 99).

10. Optional, if your pet is very active: Measure and cut 2 lengths of elastic to loop around each front leg and under the armpit, attaching both ends of each elastic piece to the costume band. If desired, create elastic bands for the back legs also. **(Diagram D)**

Diagram D

11. Glue a large pompom to each end of the straight chenille stem. Wrap the center of the stem around the headband three turns and glue securely in place. Or glue the pompoms to either end of the curly chenille stem and wrap the stem around your pet's head, under his chin and twist together on top to fit.

Note: Since the body shape of your cat or dog can vary, it is best to try the costume on your pet several times while creating the costume to make sure the placement of the hook and loop tape, elastic and wings are correct before gluing or sewing in place. Also, make sure that piece A is not too tight and that your pet can easily expand his ribcage to breathe. The optional elastic loops should fit tautly but comfortably.

(Photo permission Barb Zurawski)

Stamp ribbon with seasonal images and textile ink. Attach hook-and-loop tape closures. Note: Make sure the ribbon does not have decorative metallic or wire edging. Used with permission 2001© Hero Arts Rubber.

Creative Options:

● Emboss silver or gold spider webs on black ribbon.

● Add decorative pumpkin buttons or charms to the collar.

● Sponge black ink along a cloud pattern to create spooky clouds.

● For an even easier ribbon collar, just use a pre-printed ribbon instead of stamping the design.

● Glue or stitch contrasting trim to the long edges of the ribbon.

● Stamp a ribbon collar for each holiday or season, using appropriate images and colors.

Halloween Bandana

Following the instructions on page 7, make this easy, slip-on bandana. Or make one of the stamped collars shown on pages 40-45 in Halloween colors for your spooky pet!

(Photo permission Barb Zurawski)

Fleecy Christmas Neckwear

Supplies for all three pieces:

1 yard of Berber fleece
Scrap of white felt

Craft cord in color of your choice

Hook and loop tape
Small jingle bells (6 or 10 mm)

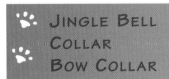

JINGLE BELL
COLLAR
BOW COLLAR

1. Cut a (2", 3", 4") wide fleece strip to the correct measurement (see page 7 on how to measure). Fold the strip in half lengthwise RST.

2. Stitch the 2 short sides and the long edge, leaving a 2" opening to turn. Turn RSO. Hand-stitch the opening shut. Sew a matching 1" strip of hook and loop tape to both ends. Sew jingle bells on as shown.

3. For a bow collar, omit jingle bells and measure a rectangular piece for the bow as follows: 2 times the width of the strip in Step 1 by the length of the cat or dog's neck. Fold in half widthwise RST to make a rectangular bow. Stitch around the 3 sides, leaving a 2" opening to turn. Turn RSO.

4. Cut a (3/4", 1", 1-1/2") wide strip the length of the bow's shorter measurement (Diagram D). Wrap the strip tightly around the center of the bow and hand-stitch. (Diagram E.) Hand-stitch the bow to the collar or slip the collar through the loop on the back of the bow.

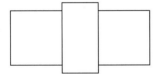

Diagram D

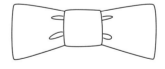

Diagram E

Creative Options:

● Make a bandana with a Christmas theme or using one of the patterns on page 111.

● Make a second bandana from the leftover triangle and give as a gift.

● Stitch the two triangles RST for a super-thick bandana.

● Make a bow collar using other seasonal colors, prints or fabrics.

CAT CHRISTMAS STOCKING

1/4 yard black metallic felt *
Craft cord **
Scraps of gray shaggy felt *
Fiberfill
Fabric glue ***
Pompoms: three 1/4" pink and six
5mm black ****

* Stormy Gray J68 Rainbow Shaggy Felt, Blush
Pink Rainbow Plush Felt and Deep Space
Black FlashFelt (Kunin Felt)
** Solid Magenta 55032 Needleloft Craft Cord
(Uniek)
*** Gem-Tac or Fabri-Tac Permanent Adhesive
(Beacon Chemical Co.)
**** Fibre-Craft

1. Enlarge the stocking and cuff pattern pieces on pages 110 and 111. Cut out fabric and sew the stocking.

2. Cut out 3 gray mice, using the mouse pattern. Sew a long gathering stitch around the edge of each mouse and pull to gather. Stuff with fiberfill.

3. Glue or hand-sew the mice on to the stocking. Glue the cuff on. Glue on craft cord tails and pompom eyes and noses.

1/4 yard tan fuzzy felt *
Scrap of red metallic felt *
12" squares of black and white craft felt *
Pompoms **:

1 (2") brown	2 (1") white
1 (1") black	2 (1/2") black

Scrap cardboard cut 1/2" smaller than the stocking pattern.
Fabric glue **

* Fawn Brown J71 Rainbow Plush Felt; White, Lime, & Black Rainbow Classic Felt; Red FlashFelt (Kunin Felt)
** Fibre-Craft
*** Gem-Tac or Fabri-Tac Permanent Adhesive (Beacon Chemical Co.)

1. Cut out 2 tan pieces from the enlarged stocking pattern on page 111. Cut 2 tan ears and one red tongue from mouse pattern. Cut out one 1-1/2" x 6" strip of black felt for the hat brim, and two 5" x 10" black rectangles for the hat.

2. Place each black hat piece along the top edge of each stocking piece, WST. Stitch across. Place the 2 stocking pieces WST and stitch along the edges of both the stocking and the hat, leaving the top hat edge open.

3. Slip the cardboard into the stocking. Glue the ears onto the stocking, just below the hat seam line. Glue the hat brim over the seam line. Glue the 2 small black pompoms onto the white pompoms to create eyes. Create the face by gluing all the pompom facial features on the stocking, as shown.

4. Glue 1/2" x 1" wide strips of red felt onto a 1" x 33" strip of white felt for a scarf. Cut 1" long fringes on either end. Tie the scarf onto the stocking and glue or hand tack in place.

Creative Options (for both stockings):

● Cut one 1" x 4" black felt strip for a loop and hand tack to the stocking.

● Add the hat, face and scarf, or the mice to a purchased stocking.

● Decorate the hat brim with green felt holly leaves and three 1/2" red pompoms as holly berries.

● Write your pet's name or greeting on the brim or cuff, using dimensional paint or glue and glitter.

● Change the dog's ear shape or add felt features, such as spots or different colors to resemble your pet.

● Glue on cat faces or silhouette instead of mice; for a dog, use bones, or dog silhouette.

Photographing Your Pet

Capture the mood or personality of your pet in an interesting and creative way that expresses something to your audience. For instance, pick out a specific trait that your pet has, and capture him being "himself." If he will cooperate, dress up your animal and create a tongue-in-cheek photo.

Backgrounds either highlight the subject by telling a "story" or distract by being cluttered. Check through the viewfinder to determine if your background is too colorful or busy or draws your eye away from the subject. If so, either simplify or change the background or crop in tightly on the subject. If operating a manual focus, change your depth of field to blur the background, keeping only your subject in sharp focus. (Photos permission In Focus Imagery, Jeff Green)

It is easy to get great photos of your pet if you follow these tips:

🐾 You will get better expression if your pet isn't stressed or worried. By shooting in familiar, comfortable surroundings with few distractions, your pet will be more relaxed.

🐾 Use funny, unexpected sounds or squeaks to get the pet's interest and natural expression.

🐾 Some pets may be intimidated by the staring "eye" of the camera. Familiarize your pet with the camera, using positive reinforcement; try a few short practice sessions prior to the actual photo shoot.

🐾 Remember to relax and have fun!

🐾 Very dark or light dogs or cats can be difficult to photograph without losing detail or expression. One tip is to try putting your camera on manual and adjust your shutter speed down two stops.

Memory Making

A DOG DAY PHOTO ALBUM

Cover a photo album or journal cover by gluing on strips of faux fur, Berber fleece or other printed or textured fabric. Finish by adding a silhouette dog cutout and assorted decorative trims of your choice (such as pearl strands, gold craft cord, lace, buttons, or ribbons).

CRAZY CAT PHOTO ALBUM

Use colorful paper for your collage instead of fabric. Decorate with paper punch-outs, stenciling and rubber-stamped and embossed textures on paper strips. Add cut out photos and unusual 3-dimensional details such as a miniature ball of yarn.

Creative Options:

● Create a more casual cover using colored felt.

● Glue hand-torn strips of tissue paper onto the cover. Tear and glue small pieces of tissue for an overall pattern.

● Cut out images of your pet from photos and glue them onto fabric, tissue or fabric decorated album.

Use different memory making techniques and create one-of-a-kind pages to record special events, celebrations or especially endearing photos of your one-of-a-kind friend! To eliminate unattractive backgrounds, cut the images out of photos and glue them onto the memory pages in a creative collage. Add borders, phrases, or other decorative items to liven up the pages, or mount several individual photos onto a contrasting color paper and attach onto a page. Draw, stamp or stencil borders around individual photos; or simply mount a single photo onto a decorated page.

PAINTED DOG AND CAT FRAMES

Acrylic paint * in assorted colors
Unfinished, flat wood frame with a small picture opening ***
Palette to mix paints
Assorted shader and liner paintbrushes
Foam paintbrush, foam sponge wedges, kitchen sponge, scissors
Transfer paper ** and a stylus or pen to trace with

* Folk Art Acrylic paints in the following colors (Plaid Enterprises):

Dog Frame: 825 Taffy, 676 Metallic Inca Gold, 663 Metallic Solid Bronze, 664 Metallic Copper,
661 Metallic Sequin Black, 659 Metallic Pearl White, 493 Metallic Bright Red
665 Metallic Garnet Red, 666 Metallic Antique Copper, and 580 Metallic Taupe

Cat Frame: 676 Metallic Inca Gold, 659 Metallic Pearl White, 669 Metallic Periwinkle, 665 Metallic Garnet Red, 664 Metallic Copper, 661 Metallic Sequin Black, and 662 Metallic Silver Sterling
** Wax-Free Transfer Paper (Saral Paper Corp.)
*** Walnut Hollow

1. Sand the frame. Paint the entire top surface of the frame with Taffy (dog) or Gold (cat). Paint the sides Bronze (dog) or Copper (cat). Let dry.

2. For cat only: Cut a 3" long triangle shape from the kitchen sponge. Sponge Copper stripes around the top and sides of the top surface of the frame.

3. For both: Trace the eyes, nose, mouth, and ears templates from page 110 onto the frame. Paint each eye area with a mixture of Black and White, plus Bronze for dog and Periwinkle for cat, blending in White highlights and Silver shading. Outline the entire eye shape in Black. Paint the nose Black with White highlights for dog and Garnet Red for cat, with White and Black blended in to define the nostrils.

4. For cat: draw mouth lines in Black. Add a shadow within the mouth lines and along the bottom edge of the frame for a chin, using a blend of Silver, Copper, and Black. Blend Black and Silver to a soft charcoal color and carefully paint whiskers, stroking toward the frame edge to draw. Let dry.

5. For dog: paint the face, using gold with Copper, Bronze, and Antique Copper blended in to give contour and add shading. Paint the ears by blending and shading Bronze, Copper, Black and Antique Copper to define the contours. Add highlights of Gold. Paint the tongue, blending both reds and highlighting with White. Add Antique Copper spots on the muzzle. Let dry.

Creative Options:
● Draw in details such as whiskers, fur strokes, or outline eyes with a fine tip permanent brown, gray or black marker.

● Change the eye or ear shape, muzzle type, or colors to more closely resemble your own pet or breed.

● Paint in a more contemporary style, using flat color areas and/or solid black outlines.

AFTERWORD

When All is Said and Done ....

If there is just one lesson we can learn from our human-animal bond, it is that we can benefit from seeing the world through their eyes. It is my sincere wish that this book will gently remind each one of us who is owned by a special dog or cat (or several), how much better life is when we can share it with someone.

Although many of us know and believe in the importance of responsible pet ownership and training, sadly there are others who do not seem to care. The voices of animal humane organizations and the media continue to remind us of the growing numbers of abused, abandoned and neglected "throw-away" pets and the horrors of commercial puppy and kitten farms.

Pets can enrich our lives in many ways. They amuse, console, and offer companionship by sharing our homes, our joys, and even our sorrows. Each one of us can feel loved, less lonely, and less stressed when we open our hearts and share our lives with another living being. In fact, our remarkable capability to love a creature other than our own species makes us more human. Perhaps the unconditional love we experience in our pets reflects a higher power, in whose reflection we also see the best in ourselves.

(Photo courtesy Peggy Farrell-Kidd)

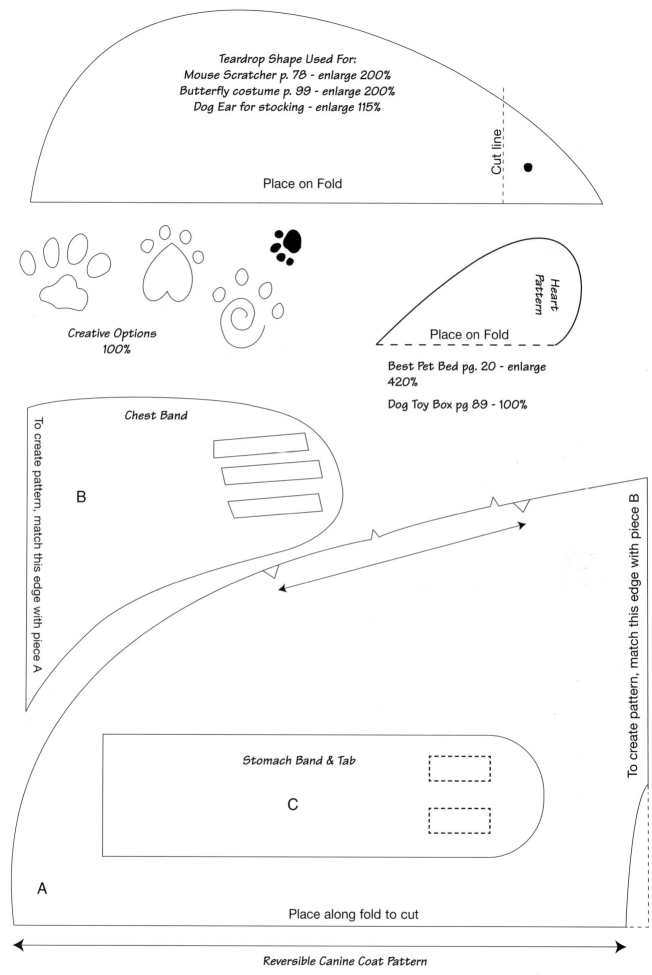

Teardrop Shape Used For:
Mouse Scratcher p. 78 - enlarge 200%
Butterfly costume p. 99 - enlarge 200%
Dog Ear for stocking - enlarge 115%

Cut line

Place on Fold

Creative Options
100%

Heart
Pattern

Place on Fold

Best Pet Bed pg. 20 - enlarge 420%

Dog Toy Box pg 89 - 100%

Chest Band

To create pattern, match this edge with piece A

B

To create pattern, match this edge with piece B

Stomach Band & Tab

C

A

Place along fold to cut

Reversible Canine Coat Pattern

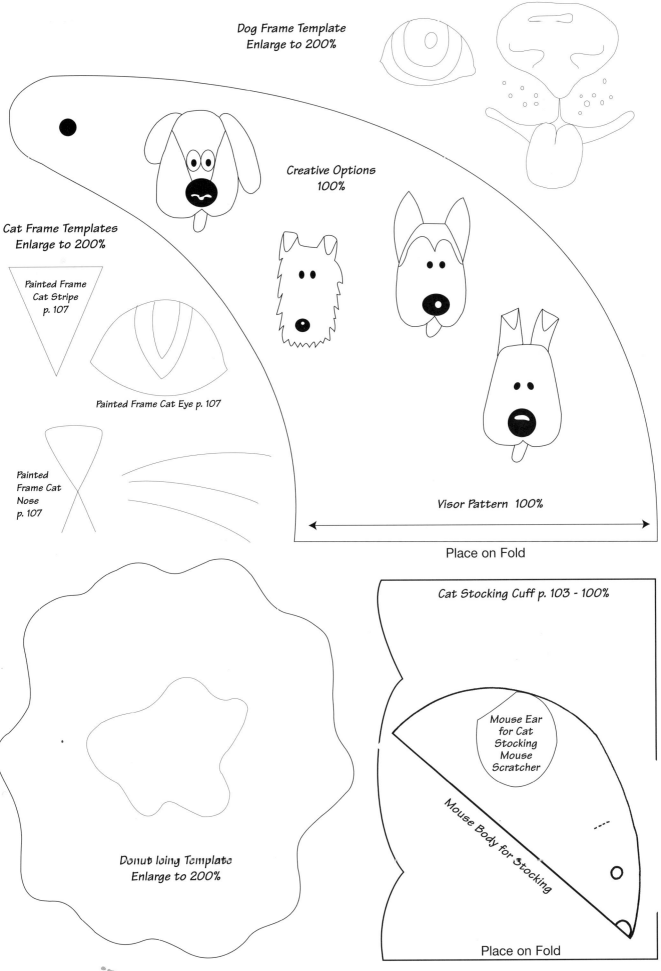

Dog Frame Template
Enlarge to 200%

Creative Options
100%

Cat Frame Templates
Enlarge to 200%

Painted Frame
Cat Stripe
p. 107

Painted Frame Cat Eye p. 107

Painted
Frame Cat
Nose
p. 107

Visor Pattern 100%

Place on Fold

Cat Stocking Cuff p. 103 - 100%

Mouse Ear
for Cat
Stocking
Mouse
Scratcher

Mouse Body for Stocking

Donut Icing Template
Enlarge to 200%

Place on Fold

THE CAT AND DOG LOVER'S IDEA BOOK

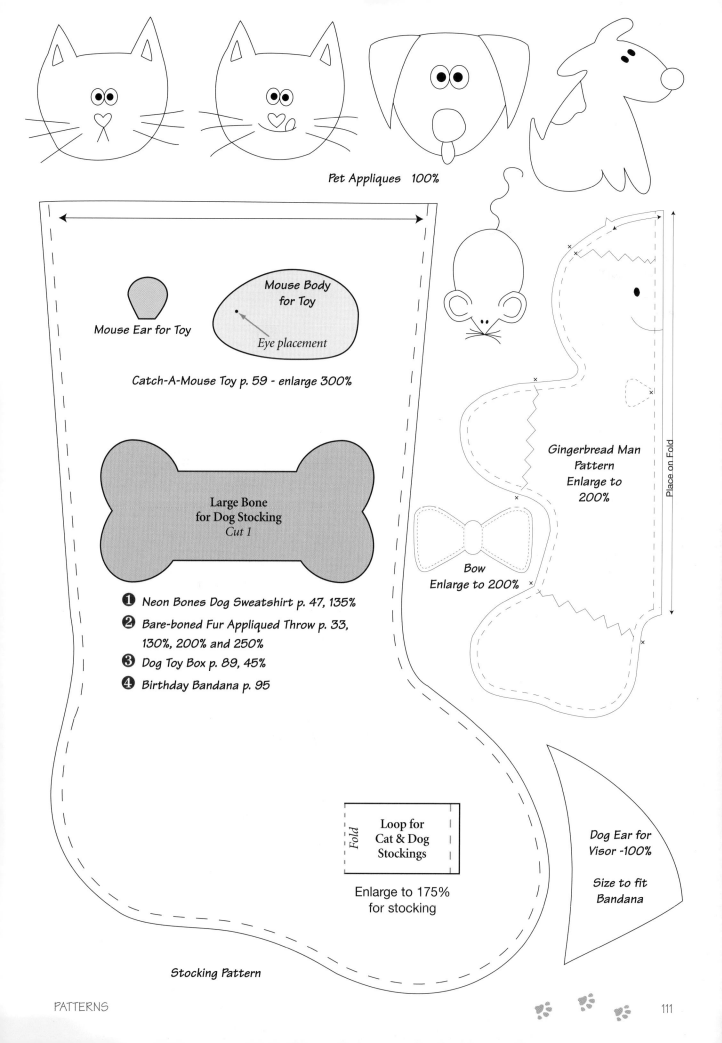

Pet Appliques   100%

Mouse Ear for Toy

Mouse Body
for Toy

Eye placement

Catch-A-Mouse Toy p. 59 - enlarge 300%

Large Bone
for Dog Stocking
Cut 1

❶ Neon Bones Dog Sweatshirt p. 47, 135%

❷ Bare-boned Fur Appliqued Throw p. 33,
   130%, 200% and 250%

❸ Dog Toy Box p. 89, 45%

❹ Birthday Bandana p. 95

Gingerbread Man
Pattern
Enlarge to
200%

Place on Fold

Bow
Enlarge to 200%

Fold

Loop for
Cat & Dog
Stockings

Enlarge to 175%
for stocking

Dog Ear for
Visor -100%

Size to fit
Bandana

Stocking Pattern

Pet Information Resources

Registries for individual breed and household pet clubs

The American Kennel Club (AKC)
260 Madison Avenue, 4th Floor
5580 Centerview Drive, Suite 200
New York, NY
        or:
Raleigh, NC 27606-3390
Phone: 919-233-9767
Fax: 919-233-3627
http://www.akc.org/
The largest, most recognized purebred dog registry in the United States

Cat Fanciers' Federation (CFF)
P.O. Box 661
Gratis, OH 45330
Phone: 937-787-9009
Fax: 937-787-4290
www.cffinc.org
A feline registry with clubs and judges in the Midwest and Eastern portions of the United States

The United Kennel Club (UKC)
100 E. Kilgore Road
Kalamazoo, MI 49002-5584
616-343-9020
www.ukcdogs.com
The second oldest and largest all-breed dog registry in the United States

The Cat Fanciers Association (CFA)
P.O. Box 1005
Manasquan, NJ 08736-0805
Phone: 732-528-9797
Fax: 732-528-7391
www.cfainc.org
The world's largest registry of pedigreed cats with clubs, shows, and judges.

The American Cat Fanciers Association (ACFA)
P.O. Box 203
Point Lookout, MO 65726
Phone: 417-334-5430
Fax: 417-334-5540
www.acfacat.com
Purebred and non-purebred cat organization with shows, judges, and regional clubs.

The International Cat Association (TICA)
P.O. Box 2684
Harlingen, TX 78551
Fax 956-428-8047
Phone: 956-428-8046
An international feline registry with clubs, shows, and judges for purebred and non-purebred cats.

The Delta Society
289 Perimeter Road East
Renton, WA 98055-1329
Phone: 425-226-7357
E-mail: deltasociety@cis.com-puserve.com
www.deltasociety.org
Service organization involved with therapy dogs and other animals

The American Society for the Prevention of Cruelty to Animals (ASPCA)
424 East 92nd Street
New York, NY 10128
Phone: 212-876-7700
www.aspca.org

The Humane Society of the United States (National Headquarters)
2100 L Street NW
Washington, DC 20037
Phone: 202-452-1100
www.hsus.org

The National Association of Professional Pet Setters (NAPPS)
10030 15th Street, NW
Suite 870
Washington, DC 20005
Phone: 800-296-PETS
www.petsitters.org

Resources for Traveling with Pets

National Association of Professional Pet Sitters
1200 G Street NW
Suite 760
Washington, DC 20005
www.petsitters.org
Phone: 800-296-7387 (referral line)

Pet Sitters International
418 E. King St.
King, NC 27021
www.petsit.com
Phone: 800-268-7487 (referral line)

American Boarding Society
Phone: 719-591-1113 (contact line)
www.abka.com

Best Friends Pet Resort Chain
Phone: 888-367-7387

Related Websites
Cat Writers Association (CWA)
www.Catwriters.org

Cat Fanciers Web Site
Includes information and links on cat breed rescue
www.fanciers.com/

Save A Pet Online
The largest index of animal rescue organizations with Web pages
www.ecn.purdue.edu/~laird/animal_rescue/

Pet Welcome
www.petswelcome.com